This book is brought to you by:

hackneyandjones.com

Writers and Publishers of fiction and non-fiction.

Scan QR Code

Copyright © 2024 by Hackney and Jones. All rights reserved.

No part of this book may be reproduced in any form or by any electronic or mechanical means, including information storage and retrieval systems, without written permission from the authors, except for the use of brief quotations in a book review.

CONTENTS

INTRODUCTION:	1
WHAT IS A MEMOIR?	13
WHAT MAKES A GREAT MEMOIR?	28
YOUR FAVOURITE 5	35
PICKING YOUR MEMOIR	41
ARE YOU READY TO WRITE YOUR MEMOIR?	44
WHAT (EXACTLY) IS YOUR MEMOIR ABOUT?	48
YOUR IDEAL READER	63
THE INCITING EVENT	70
EVERYDAY LIFE 2-3 YEARS BEFORE THE INCITING EVENT	78

CONTENTS

YOUR CHILDHOOD	85
THE 12 STEPS	91
FIRST, NEXT AND LAST...	96
YOUR TITLE AND SUB-TITLE	101
YOUR LOGLINE	105
WRITING YOUR MEMOIR OUTLINE	109
THE WALLOP SCENE	113
WRITE YOUR MEMOIR IN FULL	118
EDITING	120
YOUR NEXT STEPS	125

CONTENTS

YOUR TURN PAGES

YOUR TURN 1	130
YOUR TURN 2	132
YOUR TURN 3	136
YOUR TURN 4	138
YOUR TURN 5	140
YOUR TURN 6	144
YOUR TURN 7	146
YOUR TURN 8	148
YOUR TURN 9	150
YOUR TURN 10	152

CONTENTS

	YOUR TURN 11	154
	YOUR TURN 12	158
	YOUR TURN 13	162
	YOUR TURN 14	165
YOUR TURN PAGES	YOUR TURN 15	170
	YOUR TURN 16	177
	YOUR TURN 17	180
	YOUR TURN 18	220
RESOURCES		222

INTRODUCTION

EMBARK ON YOUR ADVENTURE!

INTRODUCTION

WHY ARE YOU HERE?

Welcome!
You're here because you want to write your memoir. You've come to the right place.

Maybe you have funny stories, exciting adventures, or important lessons you've learned?

In this workbook, you will learn how to write these stories so that others can enjoy them too.

You're about to embark on an exciting (and important) personal journey.

OUR MISSION

In our memoir writing guide, we will help you to write your story step by step, making it easier and enjoyable without it feeling overwhelming.

WHAT HAS BEEN HOLDING YOU BACK?

Fear of perfection? - confidence
Don't know where to start? - the steps
Don't have any ideas? - inspiration

There is no such thing as perfection - done is better than perfect. But there is a road map that will help you.

We will give you ALL the steps - so there is no need to worry at all.

INTRODUCTION

WHAT THIS WORKBOOK IS

This workbook is a 'build' course that takes you step by step through a streamlined process to create a gripping memoir that you will be proud to pass around to your friends and family.

WHAT THIS WORKBOOK IS NOT

This workbook is not full of 'fluff' just talking about memoirs. We are here to get your memoir DONE.

HOW WE WILL DO IT

We will use this structure to create your memoir.

The Structure of Your Memoir
'The Building Blocks'

- Title
- Sub-Title
- Wallop Scene
- Childhood
- Everyday life before
- Inciting Event
- Chapters
- Conclusion

We will give you all the necessary information for you to complete each part of the structure.

INTRODUCTION

WHY DO WE USE A STRUCTURE AND NOT JUST WRITE AND SEE WHAT HAPPENS?

This workbook is about our process that works. So we didn't want to recommend a method that hasn't worked for us.

We created this structure to help ease all the problems and reasons why people may start but NOT finish their memoir - (we use structures in our creative writing lives also).

Using a solid structure or outline when writing your memoir can be very beneficial for several reasons:

GUARANTEED QUALITY

Clear focus: Having an outline helps us stay focused on the main themes and events we want to share. This ensures our story remains coherent and doesn't stray off-topic.

Consistent flow: An outline helps us organise our thoughts and ideas in a logical sequence. This makes our memoir easier to read and understand, providing a smoother experience for the reader.

Balanced content: By planning ahead, we can make sure each part of our memoir receives the right amount of attention. We avoid spending too much time on less important details while ensuring the key moments are fully explored.

Identifying gaps: An outline allows us to see if there are any parts of our story that need more detail or explanation. This way, we can fill in any gaps and make our memoir more complete.

INTRODUCTION

WHY DO WE USE A STRUCTURE AND NOT JUST WRITE AND SEE WHAT HAPPENS?

EASE OF WRITING

Guided writing process: With an outline, we have a clear guide to follow as we write. This makes the process less overwhelming because we know exactly what to write about in each section.

Efficient use of time: Planning our memoir with an outline saves time in the long run. We can avoid the need for extensive revisions later on because we've already organised our ideas logically.

Overcoming writer's block: When we know what to write about next, it's easier to keep going. An outline provides direction, helping us overcome any moments when we feel stuck.

We all want to be able to share our stories and memories with others.

It's fun to remember important times in our lives and tell people about them.

REMEMBER

Your memoir could change lives. Memoirs could save lives.

So it's important to get it right.

INTRODUCTION

THE STRUGGLE

You are currently struggling with figuring out how to start writing your memoir and how to make your stories interesting and meaningful.

You may also be struggling with how to plan it out and stay motivated while writing it.

Would that be right?

It's hard to:

- Know where to begin your story.
- Decide which memories are the most important to include.
- Find the right words to describe your experiences.
- Keep your writing interesting and engaging for readers.
- Organise your stories in a way that makes sense.
- Stay motivated to keep writing and finish your memoir.

We will solve all of that throughout this workbook.

We have been where you are right now, we know exactly how you feel.

You may be thinking:

"I'm not a good writer, so I won't be able to do this."

"My life isn't interesting enough for a memoir."

"I don't have enough time to write a whole book."

INTRODUCTION

WE WILL...

Overcome the belief of not being a good writer by providing easy-to-follow writing techniques and exercises that improve your storytelling skills over time.

Help you discover the uniqueness in your life experiences, guiding you to find compelling angles and perspectives that make your memoir engaging and meaningful.

Break down the writing process into manageable steps, allowing you to progress at your own pace and fit writing into your schedule, making it achievable even with a busy lifestyle.

WHO THIS IS FOR

This workbook is for individuals who are ready and willing to delve into their life experiences and transform them into a compelling memoir.

It's ideal for those who are eager to share their stories with authenticity and passion, ready to engage in the process of reflection and storytelling.

WHAT WE WILL COVER

- **Your experience with memoirs:** Discovering memorable life moments.
- **What to write about:** Choosing meaningful memories to share.
- **Picking your memoir:** Selecting the story that defines you.
- **Being ready:** Feeling prepared to write your personal story.
- **Inciting event:** Recalling the moment that changed everything.
- **The transformation:** Showing how you've grown and changed.
- **12 step journey:** Guiding you through each memoir-writing stage.
- **First, next, and then...:** Organise your memories in chronological order.
- **Title:** Crafting a captivating name for your memoir.
- **Your outline:** Planning the structure of your memoir chapters.
- **Write your memoir:** Putting your memories into words.
- **Editing your memoir:** Polishing your story to perfection.

WHO ARE WE?

Hi, I'm Claire Hackney and I am a former teacher turned full-time novelist and publisher from Cheshire, England. My background in teaching English, Drama, and Media Studies fuels my storytelling passion.

My intrigue for history finds a home in my work, particularly in our 1950s-inspired novels (Meet Me at 10 etc.). Beyond this, I'm set to embark on an exciting path, including finishing the upcoming DI Rachel Morrison crime thriller series.

Find me at:

TWITTER: @ClaireHac
INSTAGRAM: @clairehackneyauthor
WEBSITE: hackneyandjones.com

Hi, I'm Vicky Jones and I'm from Essex, England. I joined the Royal Navy at 20 but felt something was missing. So, I decided to make a bold list of 300 things to do, and my life transformed, especially after attending a writing group to help me write a novel which went on to become a bestseller.

I have also written songs for iTunes and YouTube. One of my songs, "House of Cards," is centred around the theme of bullying. I also co-wrote 'Meet Me at 10' with Claire, a book which deals with controversial societal issues.

I love to travel and have been to around 50 countries - so far! I have also also gained a psychology and criminology degree from The Open University.

Although now living in Cheshire, I keep ties with my Essex roots.

My journey is all about being creative, brave, and discovering myself.

Find me at:

TWITTER: @VickyJones7
INSTAGRAM: @vickyt.jones
WEBSITE: hackneyandjones.com

OUR WRITING JOURNEY

WE HAVE WRITTEN FICTION AND NON-FICTION BOOKS!

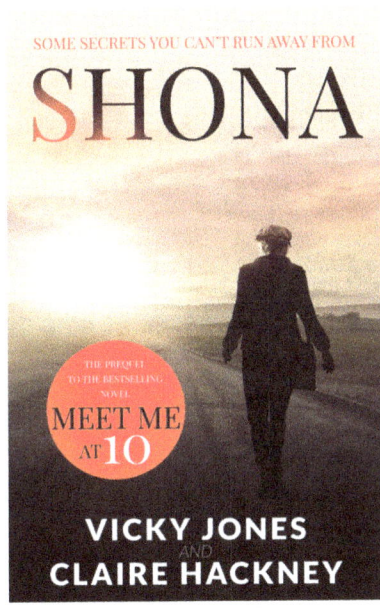
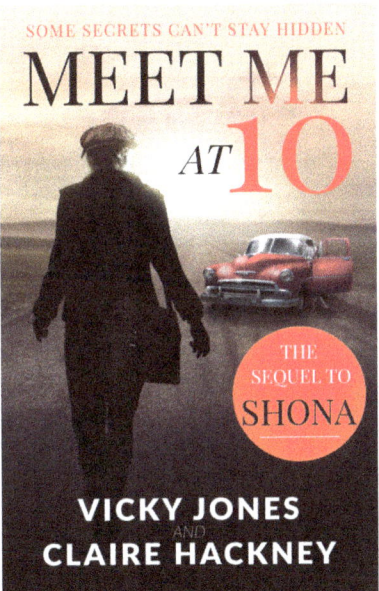
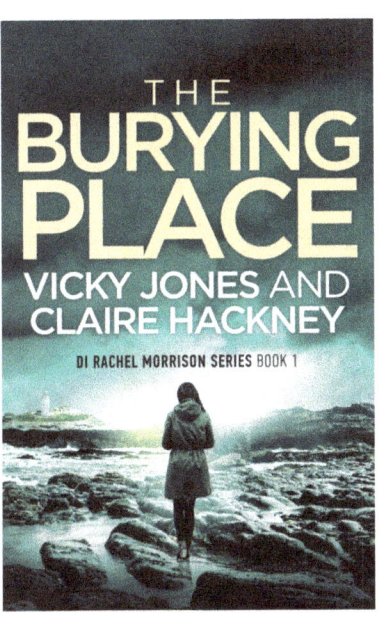

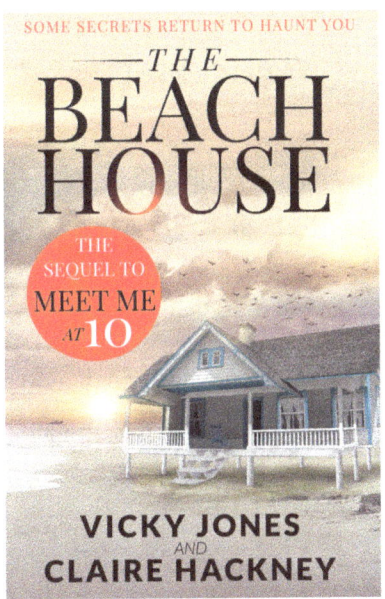

OUR WRITING JOURNEY

WE HAVE WRITTEN FICTION AND NON-FICTION BOOKS!

Get the code to craft irresistible short stories from scratch with guaranteed quality every time.

For beginners or pro writers who are excited to discover a brand new way to elevate their storytelling.

Get more done, finish every idea you start.

Would you love to write irresistible stories for kids – on repeat?

Picture children all over reading your stories with a beaming smile on their face eager to turn the page and bug their parents to get all of your books!

To do this on repeat, you need a plan.
A successful plan, right?

Look no further than 'Write Awesome Stories for Kids'.

A one-stop-shop roadmap that takes you from blank page to binge-worthy stories for children.

OUR WRITING JOURNEY

> Years ago, I wrote a deeply personal memoir called 'Project Me, Project You'.
>
> It focused on my struggle with depression and how writing and completing things on my Bucket List got rid of my depression.
>
> We created our process to help us, and now it will help you write your memoir faster, better, and easier.

OUR WRITING JOURNEY

OUR WHY

We wanted to help others like you to achieve a heartfelt memoir every time without struggling to find the right words or losing motivation along the way.

We believe everybody has a story in them... What's yours?

WHERE YOUR MEMOIR COULD TAKE YOU

You could:

- Inspire others with your courageous journey.
- Preserve cherished family stories for generations.
- Share wisdom and life lessons with a wider audience.
- Connect deeply with readers through shared experiences.
- Capture and celebrate significant milestones in your life.

This could lead to opportunities for speaking engagements, book signings, and sharing your wisdom with larger audiences.

Let's begin shall we...?

WHAT IS A MEMOIR?

WHAT IS A MEMOIR?

A memoir is a type of autobiographical writing that focuses on a specific period or theme in a person's life. It typically offers personal reflections and insights, often highlighting significant events, relationships, or experiences.

Example: "The Glass Castle" by Jeannette Walls is a memoir that recounts the author's unconventional and poverty-stricken upbringing with her dysfunctional family. Through vivid storytelling, Walls reflects on her childhood struggles and the impact they had on her life.

WHAT IT IS NOT

A memoir is not a work of fiction, but rather it is a form of nonfiction that recounts real-life events and experiences from the author's perspective.

Additionally, a memoir is not the same as an autobiography.

While both genres delve into the author's life, a memoir typically focuses on a specific aspect or period of the author's life, whereas an autobiography aims to provide a comprehensive account of the author's entire life from birth to the present.

WHAT IS A MEMOIR?

FAMOUS MEMOIRS

"The Diary of a Young Girl" by Anne Frank

Theme: Life during the Holocaust

Specifics: This memoir is the real-life diary of Anne Frank, a Jewish girl who went into hiding with her family during the Nazi occupation of the Netherlands. Written while they were concealed in a secret annexe, Anne's diary provides a poignant and personal insight into the fears, hopes, and daily struggles of a young girl during one of history's darkest times. The diary ends abruptly when the family is betrayed and arrested.

"Becoming" by Michelle Obama

Theme: Personal and professional growth

Specifics: In "Becoming," former First Lady Michelle Obama shares her life story, from her childhood in Chicago to her years as an executive balancing work and motherhood, and finally to her time spent at the world's most famous address. The memoir provides an intimate look at her experiences and challenges, both personal and public, offering readers insight into her journey of self-discovery and the values that shaped her. Michelle Obama reflects on the trials and triumphs that defined her path and her role in history as the first African American First Lady of the United States.

WHAT IS A MEMOIR?

WHAT IS THE DIFFERENCE BETWEEN A MEMOIR AND AN AUTOBIOGRAPHY?

A memoir and an autobiography both tell the story of someone's life, but they have some key differences:

Focus: A memoir focuses on specific events or periods in the author's life, highlighting particular experiences and memories. An autobiography covers the author's entire life, from birth to the present.

Detail: A memoir is more detailed about certain events and is usually more personal and emotional. An autobiography is more factual and includes a broader overview of the author's life.

Length: Memoirs are often shorter because they focus on specific parts of the author's life. Autobiographies are usually longer since they cover the whole life story.

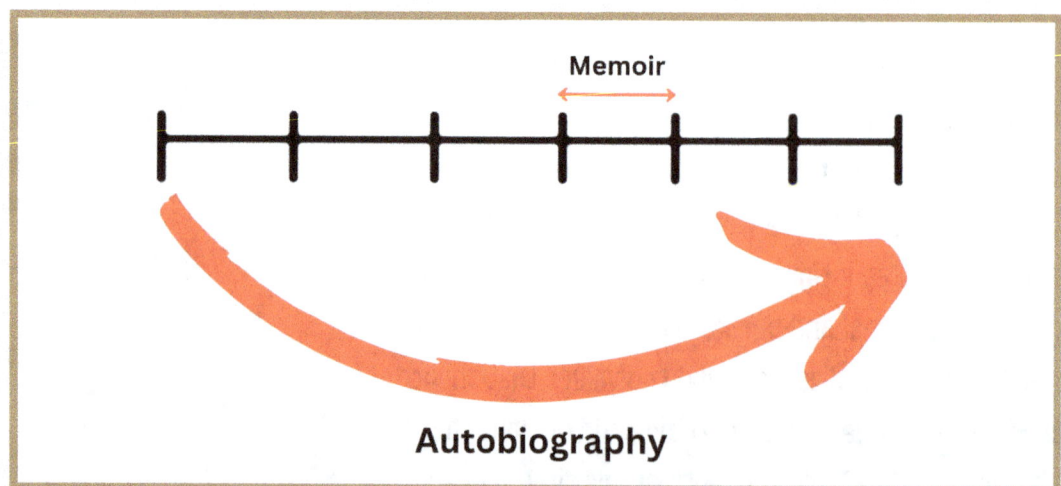

WHAT IS A MEMOIR?

HOW DO I CHOOSE WHAT TO INCLUDE IN MY MEMOIR?

Focus on significant events, experiences, relationships, or themes that shaped you or had a profound impact on your life.

Choose moments that contribute to a coherent narrative or theme you want to explore.

WHAT MAKES A GRIPPING AND ENGAGING MEMOIR THAT READERS LOVE?

A gripping and engaging memoir typically incorporates several key aspects that resonate with readers on a personal level.

- Conflict.
- Overcoming challenges.
- Emotions.
- Transformation.
- Universal themes.
- Honesty and authenticity.

WHY READERS LOVE 'CONFLICT'

Engagement: Conflict drives the narrative forward and keeps readers engaged, wondering how the situation will be resolved.

Relatability: Everyone experiences conflict in their lives. Seeing how others handle it helps readers feel connected to the story.

Character development: Conflict reveals a person's character, strengths, and weaknesses, making the memoir's protagonist more complex and interesting.

WHAT IS A MEMOIR?

WHY READERS LOVE 'OVERCOMING CHALLENGES'

Inspiration: Stories of overcoming adversity inspire readers to face their own challenges with courage and determination.

Hope: Knowing that someone else has navigated difficult times successfully provides hope and encouragement.

Personal growth: These stories often show significant personal growth, which can be motivating and affirming for readers.

WHY READERS LOVE 'EMOTIONS'

Connection: Emotions help readers connect deeply with the writer's experiences and feelings.

Authenticity: Sharing emotions makes the story feel real and genuine, enhancing its impact.

Empathy: Emotions allow readers to empathise with the writer, fostering a sense of shared human experience.

WHY READERS LOVE 'TRANSFORMATION'

Journey: Readers enjoy following a person's journey from one state of being to another, often involving personal growth or change.

Resolution: Transformation provides a sense of resolution and closure, making the story satisfying.

Learning: Seeing how someone transforms through their experiences can offer valuable life lessons and insights.

WHAT IS A MEMOIR?

WHY READERS LOVE 'UNIVERSAL THEMES'

Relatability: Universal themes like love, loss, and identity resonate with a wide audience because they are common human experiences.

Meaning: These themes often explore the deeper meaning of life, prompting readers to reflect on their own lives.

Connection: Shared themes help readers feel a sense of connection with the writer and other readers, fostering a sense of community.

WHY READERS LOVE 'HONESTY AND AUTHENTICITY'

Trust: Honesty builds trust between the writer and the reader, making the story more credible.

Raw and real: Authenticity brings out the raw and real aspects of the writer's life, which can be compelling and moving.

Courage: It takes courage to be honest and authentic, and readers appreciate and admire this bravery.

WHAT IS A MEMOIR?

HOW CAN WE DO THIS?

INCLUDE:

The main thing that happens in each scene:

- This anchors the scene in a specific event or moment, providing a focal point that drives the narrative forward and keeps readers engaged.

Using the 5 senses: (See, hear, touch, taste and smell)

- Describing the setting using all five senses immerses readers in the environment, making it vivid and tangible. It creates a sensory experience that enhances the realism and authenticity of the scene.

Interesting characters:

- Characters bring the scene to life through their personalities, motivations, and interactions. Their presence adds complexity and dynamics, fostering empathy and interest from readers.

Action – What actually happened step by step:

- Detailing the actions and events in sequence creates a sense of immediacy and progression. It moves the narrative forward while maintaining clarity and coherence.

Authentic dialogue (What was said and by whom):

- Dialogue reveals characters' relationships, emotions, and conflicts through their words and interactions. It adds authenticity and depth to their personalities, driving the narrative and revealing insights.

WHAT IS A MEMOIR?

HOW CAN WE DO THIS?

INCLUDE:

Conflict (What went wrong and why):

- Conflict introduces tension and challenges that characters must navigate. It creates stakes, raises questions, and drives the narrative forward by exploring obstacles and their consequences.

Emotions (What did I feel and why):

- Exploring emotions enriches the narrative by revealing the impact of events on the narrator and characters. It fosters empathy from readers and deepens their connection to the story.

My internal thoughts:

- Internal thoughts provide insights into the narrator's reflections, perspectives, and personal growth. They offer introspection and deepen the reader's understanding of the narrator's journey.

Resolution - How did this scene end?:

- The resolution brings closure to the scene, addressing the conflict or situation introduced earlier. It reveals the outcomes of actions taken and their significance to the narrative and characters.

Lesson/s I learned and why:

- Lessons learned convey the memoir's deeper meaning and personal growth. They offer reflections on experiences, and insights into life's complexities, and connect the narrative to universal truths.

HOW WILL I REMEMBER TO INCLUDE ALL OF THIS IN EVERY MAJOR SCENE?

By using our structure/framework - we've got you covered. You will include all the important elements without having to worry. It is important that you follow EVERY STEP so that you don't miss out on something important.

WHAT IS A MEMOIR?

COMMON QUESTIONS ABOUT MEMOIR WRITING

How long should my memoir be?

- Aim for a memoir length that feels natural for your story, typically ranging from 60,000 to 100,000 words. Focus on quality and clarity rather than meeting a specific word count.

How many chapters should my memoir have?

- The number of chapters can vary widely based on your story's structure and pacing. A typical memoir may have anywhere from 10 to 30 chapters. Let your narrative flow naturally, and divide chapters based on key events or themes.

What themes should I focus on?

- Choose themes that resonate with your experiences and central message.

- Common themes include resilience, personal growth, overcoming adversity, family dynamics, identity, and self-discovery.

Or...

- Family dynamics.
- Love and relationships.
- Travel and exploration.
- Loss and grief.
- Career and ambition.
- Mental health.
- Social justice.
- Spirituality and belief.

WHAT IS A MEMOIR?

THEMES AND IDEAS FOR A MEMOIR

Specific examples within each theme (to give you ideas):

1. Family Dynamics:

- Growing up in a blended family: Navigating relationships with step-siblings and step-parents while finding a sense of belonging.

- Dealing with a family secret: The impact of discovering a hidden truth about your family and how it changes your relationships.

- Caring for ageing parents: The challenges and rewards of becoming a caregiver for your elderly parents and the effect on family roles.

2. Love and Relationships:

- First love and heartbreak: Experiencing the joy and pain of your first romantic relationship and how it shaped your views on love.

- Navigating a long-distance relationship: The trials and triumphs of maintaining a relationship across great distances.

- Rebuilding after infidelity: The process of healing and rebuilding trust after a partner's betrayal

WHAT IS A MEMOIR?

THEMES AND IDEAS FOR A MEMOIR

Specific examples within each theme (to give you ideas):

3. Travel and Exploration

- **Solo backpacking journey:** Personal growth and self-discovery while travelling alone through foreign countries.

- **Living abroad:** The cultural adjustments and adventures of moving to and living in a different country.

- **Unexpected adventures:** Life-changing experiences during a trip that didn't go as planned, such as getting lost or encountering unique situations

4. Loss and Grief

- **Losing a loved one:** Coping with the death of a close family member or friend and the grieving process.

- **Miscarriage and infertility:** The emotional journey of dealing with miscarriage or the struggle to conceive.

- **Life after divorce:** The pain of ending a marriage and the path to rebuilding your life and identity afterwards.

WHAT IS A MEMOIR?

THEMES AND IDEAS FOR A MEMOIR

Specific examples within each theme (to give you ideas):

5. Career and Ambition

- **Changing careers:** The challenges and rewards of leaving a secure job to pursue a passion or dream career.

- **Starting a business:** The ups and downs of launching and growing your own business from scratch.

- **Overcoming workplace discrimination:** Personal experiences of facing and overcoming discrimination in the workplace.

6. Mental Health

- **Living with depression:** The daily struggles and triumphs of managing depression and finding ways to cope.

- **Recovering from addiction:** The journey through addiction, recovery, and the impact on your life and relationships.

- **Navigating anxiety:** How anxiety affects your daily life and the strategies you've developed to manage it.

WHAT IS A MEMOIR?

THEMES AND IDEAS FOR A MEMOIR

Specific examples within each theme (to give you ideas):

7. Social Justice

- **Activism and advocacy:** Personal stories of fighting for a cause, such as civil rights, environmental justice, or gender equality.

- **Experiencing injustice:** First-hand accounts of dealing with systemic racism, sexism, or other forms of discrimination.

- **Community organising:** The challenges and successes of working to create change within your community.

8. Spirituality and Belief

- **Spiritual awakening:** A transformative experience that led to a deeper understanding of your spiritual beliefs.

- **Leaving a religion:** The emotional and intellectual journey of leaving a long-held religious faith.

- **Interfaith marriage:** Navigating the complexities and joys of a marriage between two different faiths and how it affects family life.

WHAT IS A MEMOIR?

HOW DO I START MY MEMOIR?

- Begin with a compelling hook that draws readers into your story.

- Consider starting with a significant moment, an intriguing question, or a vivid description that sets the tone for your memoir.

HOW HONEST SHOULD I BE?

- Strive for honesty while considering the impact on yourself and others involved.

- It's crucial to be truthful about your experiences while respecting privacy and sensitivities.

- Transparency strengthens your narrative's authenticity.

HOW DO I HANDLE WRITING ABOUT PEOPLE WHO ARE STILL ALIVE?

- Respect privacy and consider how others might perceive their portrayal.

- Obtain consent if discussing sensitive or personal matters involving living individuals.

- Alter details or use pseudonyms to protect identities if necessary.

HOW DO I KEEP MY READERS ENGAGED?

- Maintain a compelling narrative pace by balancing introspection with action and dialogue.

- Show vulnerability and emotional depth, and use vivid descriptions to immerse readers in your world.

- End chapters with hooks to encourage continuous reading. Eg:

> "Little did I know, the journey ahead would challenge me in ways I never imagined. As I closed the door behind me, I couldn't shake the feeling that this decision would change everything..."

By following our method, you will solve all your worries and be left with an expertly told personal story people will love to read.

WHAT MAKES A GREAT MEMOIR?

WHAT MAKES A GREAT MEMOIR?

LEARNING WHAT THE BESTSELLERS DO

You will stop readers from switching off or giving your memoir a bad review and instead you will feel super confident at knowing your memoir will hit the mark by learning what the bestsellers do so you can emulate their success without feeling confused!

Before we start writing our memoir, isn't it better to know what our readers like and dislike? A memoir is meant to be read by others, if not, it's a diary – simple as that. If it is meant to be read by others, shouldn't we know what they want?

HOW DO WE FIND OUT THIS INFORMATION?

The first way is by looking at reviews. Your potential readers are giving you lots of clues as to what they love. The second way is by your own experience reading memoirs.

(More on that later)

Type into Amazon search bar – 'Memoir'

Click on a memoir that has lots of reviews (Tip. if you are already clear on what you want to write your memoir about, click on a memoir that is on the same subject as yours)

Lots of reviews = lots of data for you!

Go through the 1,2,3,4 and 5 stars and make notes of 'likes and dislikes' and put them into 'buckets' that are of the same info.

(Tip – the 2,3 and 4 stars tend to give away more information to 'justify' their review which means more info for you!)

WHAT MAKES A GREAT MEMOIR?

New - Amazon now sums up the customer experience.

Using technology etc. Amazon sum of the customer experience so it is easier for you to see OVERALL what the readers like and dislike

> **Customers say**
>
> Customers find the themes inspirational, amazing, and encouraging. They also describe the writing style as beautifully written and eye-opening. Readers describe the book as a great read that shows how fragile life can be yet so strong. Opinions are mixed on the emotional tone, with some finding it full of raw emotion and real, while others find it depressing and impossible to believe.

So from this popular memoir, we can see readers LIKE:

'The theme - that it's encouraging, beautifully written and eye-opening. It's a great read.'

They DISLIKE:

'Found it depressing and impossible to believe.'

WHAT DOES THAT MEAN FOR YOU?

Readers have SAID they want the theme to be encouraging, well written, and eye-opening (great detail) BUT, they don't want it be depressing and impossible to believe.

So do you think that if you only made sure that your memoir 'fit this bill' it would improve the reader experience?

Of course!

WHAT MAKES A GREAT MEMOIR?

LET'S LOOK AT SOME MORE REVIEWS TO SEE IF WE CAN GET MORE SPECIFIC.

★★★★☆ **Incredible memoir.**
Reviewed in the United Kingdom on 6 April 2021
Verified Purchase
I have read a,lot of nature memoirs but this one will stay with me for the vivid retelling and the startling imagery. It takes the reader on a journey that at times is raw and painful and at others is uplifting and beautiful. Highly recommended.

Points for me to think about: Vivid storytelling, and imagery. Raw and painful, but uplifting and beautiful.

Although the author clearly went through a number of distressing life changes whilst living on the island and I genuinely sympathise with that (all things I myself have recently gone through, hence the excitement to read the book), I do think this book screams victim and I felt myself getting angry with the "poor me" over and over again throughout the story. Almost everyone in the book is painted negatively except the author herself. Someone above pointed out that its a bit one dimensional which I agree with as the author does not attempt to discuss why she struggled with integration, no real self reflection on any of her own flaws and i have a feeling this experience came from a place of privilege and not truly a real account of a new life in the hebrides. As a scottish woman I genuinely felt offended at her descriptions of the life and the locals and at times I myself felt frustrated with the lack of tact in handling

Points for me to think about: Don't write as a 'victim' too much, too much negativity about others, no self-reflection, no mention of her own flaws, offensive.

★★★★★ **Absolutely amazing**
Reviewed in the United Kingdom on 15 April 2021
Verified Purchase
I loved this book - I never wanted it to end! Such a talented writer; i laughed out loud at some parts and had a tear in my eye at other times. I also found the authors personal stories very inspiring - her 'can do' attitude and willingness to follow her passion, even if it meant creating waves, I just absolutely love. Thank you so much for writing such a fantastic book. Inspiring in many ways

Points for me to think about: Funny in places, sad in others. Inspiring 'can do' attitude.

WHAT MAKES A GREAT MEMOIR?

LET'S LOOK AT SOME MORE REVIEWS TO SEE IF WE CAN GET MORE SPECIFIC.

> ★★☆☆☆ **The main character of the novel was not interesting. Too self centered**
> Reviewed in the United States on 18 January 2024
> **Verified Purchase**
> I felt that the book moved at a very slow pace. The main character seemed like a selfish and self-centered person, and all she did was talk about herself and her relation to others. I did not learn anything new.

Points for me to think about: Slow pace, author seemed selfish, self-centred.

WHAT DO WE HAVE NOW?

Let's put it all into a checklist-type table to ensure that our memoir delivers EXACTLY what our readers want

DO	DON'T
The theme - that it's encouraging	Depressing
Beautifully written	Impossible to believe (far-fetched)
Eye-opening	Victim mentality throughout
Vivid storytelling/Imagery	Negative
Raw and painful	No self-reflection
Uplifting/inspiring	No mention of flaws
Can-do attitude	Offensive
Funny/sad in places	Boring

WHAT MAKES A GREAT MEMOIR?

TURN BESTSELLING MEMOIR REVIEWS INTO YOUR TO-DO LIST TO ENSURE YOU HIT THE MARK EVERY TIME...

Let's put it all into a checklist-type table to ensure that our memoir delivers EXACTLY what our readers want. For the 'DON'TS' - write what the opposite would be

DO	DON'T
The theme - that it's encouraging	Depressing (Make it more cheery)
Beautifully written	Impossible to believe (far-fetched) (Make it more believable)
Eye-opening	Victim mentality throughout (Make it more about surviving)
Vivid storytelling/Imagery	Negative (Make it more of a positive experience)
Raw and painful	No self-reflection (Reflect on your own behaviour)
Uplifting/inspiring	No mention of flaws (Mention when you've been wrong)
Can-do attitude	Offensive (Ensuring it is an inclusive read - no offence)
Funny/sad in places	Boring (Make it interesting)

Use the above table as a checklist to keep you accountable and on track as you plan and write your memoir.

WHAT MAKES A GREAT MEMOIR?

KEY TAKEAWAYS

Find similar themes ('buckets'): By checking Amazon reviews and our own reading experiences, we can see what topics and stories readers like most, such as honest feelings, stories they can relate to, and exciting storytelling.

Learn from what readers didn't like: Looking at what readers didn't enjoy in reviews and thinking about our own experiences can help us avoid common mistakes like not enough details, boring parts, or writing that doesn't grab attention.

Know what readers want: Our own experiences teach us what readers expect from a great memoir, like being true to life, telling interesting stories, and sharing important lessons, so we can make a list to meet these expectations.

NOW TURN TO **PAGE 130** FOR YOUR END-OF-UNIT ACTIVITY 'YOUR TURN 1' PAGE:

'WHAT YOU LIKE AND DISLIKE ABOUT MEMOIRS'

YOUR FAVOURITE 5

YOUR FAVOURITE 5

5 IDEAS YOU COULD WRITE YOUR MEMOIR ABOUT

In this section, you will pick 5 moments in your life that had a massive impact on you so that you have a bank of options to select the best idea to write a transformational memoir your readers will love.

WHAT IS AN IMPACTFUL LIFE EVENT?

An impactful life event is something significant or powerful that happens to a person, often changing their life in a big way.

EXAMPLES OF AN IMPACTFUL LIFE EVENT: (THINK OF THE THEMES AND IDEAS PAGE)

- Moving to a new city or country.
- Starting secondary school or college.
- Passing important exams like GCSEs or A-levels.
- Getting a first job or internship.
- Travelling abroad for the first time.
- Learning to drive and getting a licence.
- Losing a close friend or family member.
- Moving away from home for the first time.
- Experiencing a significant illness or injury.
- Attending a memorable concert or event.
- Volunteering for a meaningful cause.
- Going through a divorce or separation.
- Buying a first home or moving house.
- Starting a family or becoming a parent.
- Witnessing or being involved in a major sporting event.
- Facing a natural disaster or severe weather event.
- Graduating from university or completing a degree.
- Winning an award or recognition for achievements.
- Starting a successful business or project.
- Going on a life-changing adventure or expedition.
- Meeting a personal hero or role model.
- Overcoming a fear or phobia.
- Serving in the armed forces or military.
- Learning a new skill or hobby.
- Making a significant career change.
- Starting therapy or counselling.
- Participating in a charity fundraiser or event.
- Celebrating a milestone birthday or anniversary.
- Rescuing or adopting a pet.
- Surviving a personal crisis or challenging period in life.
- Retiring from a long career or profession.
- Starting a successful nonprofit organisation or charity.
- Writing and publishing a book or significant piece of work.
- Emigrating to another country for a new start.
- Becoming a caregiver for a family member or loved one with a serious illness or disability.

YOUR FAVOURITE 5

WHY DO IMPACTING LIFE EVENTS MAKE GREAT MEMOIRS?

Impactful life events make great memoirs because they are powerful stories that show how someone overcame challenges, learned important lessons, or experienced big changes. (We know these make great memoirs!)

Readers enjoy these memoirs because they can relate to the emotions and struggles of the author, and they often find inspiration and hope in seeing how people handle difficult times.

WHY SOME IMPACTFUL LIFE EVENTS MAKE BETTER MEMOIRS THAN OTHERS

Some impactful life events make better memoirs because they are dramatic, emotional, and transformative.

They teach important lessons that many people can relate to, involving overcoming big challenges or personal growth, which makes them more interesting to readers and can have a wider impact.

WHY DOES A TRANSFORMATIONAL MEMOIR WORK BEST FOR YOUR READER?

A transformational memoir works best for readers because it tells a story of personal growth and change that they can relate to and find inspiring.

It shows how someone faced challenges, learned important lessons, and became a better person as a result.

Readers often seek these memoirs for guidance, hope, and understanding of their own lives and struggles.

THE ACTUAL TRANSFORMATION

How I went from: broke to becoming: a millionaire (transformation)
How I went from being bored in life to Climbing Mount Everest.

YOUR FAVOURITE 5

WHAT DOES TRANSFORMATION LOOK LIKE?

Transformation means a significant change or improvement from one state to another.

Here's an example:

From: Being shy and lacking confidence in social situations.

To: Becoming outgoing and comfortable speaking in public.

Real-life example: "Susan used to feel very nervous speaking in front of groups. However, after joining a public speaking club and practising regularly, she transformed from being shy to confidently delivering presentations at work and even giving speeches at community events."

OUT OF OUR PRETEND LIST OF IMPACTFUL LIFE EVENTS, WHICH WOULD MAKE THE BEST 5?

- Moving to a new city or country.
- Starting a family or becoming a parent.
- Facing a natural disaster or severe weather event.
- Surviving a personal crisis or challenging period in life.
- Emigrating to another country for a new start.

WHY?

- Moving to a new city or country.

THE TRANSFORMATION:

From: Feeling anxious and unfamiliar in a new environment.

To: Building a new life, making friends, and thriving in a different culture.

YOUR FAVOURITE 5

- Starting a family or becoming a parent.

THE TRANSFORMATION:

From: Being independent and focused on personal goals.

To: Embracing responsibility, nurturing others, and finding fulfilment in family life.

- Facing a natural disaster or severe weather event.

THE TRANSFORMATION:

From: Feeling scared and uncertain during a crisis.

To: Demonstrating resilience, helping others, and rebuilding what was lost.

- Surviving a personal crisis or challenging period in life.

THE TRANSFORMATION:

From: Struggling with pain, loss, or adversity.

To: Finding strength, learning valuable lessons, and moving forward with renewed purpose.

- Emigrating to another country for a new start.

THE TRANSFORMATION:

From: Leaving behind familiar surroundings and support systems.

To: Adapting to a new culture, pursuing new opportunities, and discovering personal growth and identity.

YOUR FAVOURITE 5

KEY TAKEAWAYS

Big events make great memoirs: Memoirs about important life events like moving to a new city or facing a crisis grab readers' interest because they show how someone grows and stays strong, which others can relate to and feel inspired by.

Transformations make better memoirs: Memoirs that show how someone changes, like overcoming challenges or seeing things differently, really connect with readers. These stories give hope and encouragement by showing how people learn and grow.

Lessons help readers: Memoirs that share lessons learned from experiences not only entertain but also teach and give power to readers. People like gaining new ideas and ways of thinking that they can use in their own lives, which makes these memoirs important and easy to remember.

NOW TURN TO <u>PAGE 132</u> FOR YOUR END-OF-UNIT ACTIVITY 'YOUR TURN 2' PAGE:

'WRITE 5 POSSIBLE IDEAS FOR YOUR MEMOIR'

PICKING YOUR MEMOIR

PICKING YOUR MEMOIR

In this section, you will feel certain that your memoir choice will be a HIT with your readers by scoring your 5 ideas out of of 10 which ensures your readers get the most value and your get the most enjoyment writing it.

WIN/WIN

YOUR READERS' EXPERIENCE IN READING YOUR MEMOIR

An author writing a memoir needs to consider the reader at all times because they want their story to be clear and meaningful to others.

(Otherwise, they will simply stop reading and that's where the 1-star reviews creep in...)

By thinking about how readers will understand and feel about their experiences, authors can make sure their memoir is engaging and relatable

Readers want to see the transformation and learn valuable lessons from memoirs because they seek inspiration and insight into overcoming challenges and growing as individuals.

They look for stories that resonate emotionally and offer meaningful takeaways they can apply to their own lives.

DOES YOUR MEMOIR SHOW CLEAR LESSONS?

Remember when you wrote how you felt about reading memoirs and when you have read reviews. Now it's your turn to consider your readers.

PICKING YOUR MEMOIR

KEY TAKEAWAYS

- **Reader value:** By scoring each memoir idea based on how much value it offers readers—such as lessons learned, you ensure your memoir will resonate deeply with your audience.

- **Transformational journey:** Evaluate each idea on its potential to showcase a transformative journey—from challenges faced to personal growth achieved—which can captivate readers and inspire them through your experiences.

- **Personal motivation:** Consider your own enthusiasm and passion for each idea. Writing a memoir that genuinely interests and excites you will ensure authenticity and depth, enhancing the overall quality and impact of your book.

NOW TURN TO <u>PAGE 136</u> FOR YOUR END-OF-UNIT ACTIVITY 'YOUR TURN 3' PAGE:

'ANSWER THE FOLLOWING QUESTIONS ABOUT EACH OF YOUR 5 MEMOIR IDEAS'

ARE YOU READY TO WRITE YOUR MEMOIR?

ARE YOU READY TO WRITE YOUR MEMOIR

ARE YOU IN THE RIGHT PLACE TO WRITE ABOUT YOUR EXPERIENCE?)

In this section, you will feel confident that you are READY and can focus on writing a memoir to be proud of by completing the I'm ready statement that ensures you have everything in place.

WHY DO YOU NEED TO BE READY TO WRITE YOUR MEMOIR?

You need to be ready to write your memoir because it requires you to reflect deeply on your life experiences, be emotionally prepared to share personal stories, and have the motivation and commitment to see the writing process through to completion.

Your memoir might unearth deep emotions, memories of trauma, or difficult experiences that you've buried or not fully processed.

Writing about these can bring healing and understanding, but it's important to be prepared for the emotional impact and to take care of yourself during the process

HAS ENOUGH TIME GONE BY?

Allowing enough time and processing before writing a memoir makes it better because it gives you a chance to think deeply about your experiences.

When you've had time to reflect, you can understand your feelings and thoughts more clearly.

This helps you give better advice to readers because you've learned valuable lessons and can share them with wisdom and insight gained from your experiences.

ARE YOU READY TO WRITE YOUR MEMOIR

IF IT'S TOO SOON...

If you haven't given enough time or are still processing trauma, writing a memoir may be more difficult and emotionally challenging.

Rushing to share your experiences before you've had time to reflect fully can make it harder to understand your feelings and offer meaningful insights to readers.

It's important to prioritise your emotional well-being and take the time you need to heal and gain clarity before sharing your story.

WHAT DOES 'BEING READY' LOOK LIKE?

Here are 4 ways to know you're ready...

- **Emotional readiness:** Being ready emotionally means feeling prepared to revisit and explore past experiences without being overwhelmed by strong emotions.

- **Clarity of reflection:** It involves having a clear understanding of the lessons learned from your experiences and how they have shaped your life.

- **Purpose and motivation:** Being ready includes having a strong desire and motivation to share your story for the benefit of others, whether to inspire, educate, or bring awareness.

- **Support system:** It means having a support network in place—such as friends, family, or professionals—who can provide emotional support and guidance during the writing process. (VERY IMPORTANT)

ARE YOU READY TO WRITE YOUR MEMOIR

KEY TAKEAWAYS

- Emotional readiness: Make sure you feel ready to explore your past without feeling overwhelmed by strong emotions.

- Clear reflection: Understand the lessons you've learned from your experiences and how they have shaped your life.

- Purpose and support: Have a strong motivation to share your story for others' benefit, and ensure you have support from friends, family, or professionals to help you through the process emotionally

NOW TURN TO PAGE 138 FOR YOUR END OF UNIT ACTIVITY 'YOUR TURN 4' PAGE:

'THE "I'M READY" STATEMENT'

WHAT (EXACTLY) IS YOUR MEMOIR ABOUT?

WHAT (EXACTLY) IS YOUR MEMOIR ABOUT?

IMPORTANT PARTS TO INCLUDE.

In this section, you will feel confident in knowing that your memoir hits all the important markers for your reader using our overview questions.

Plan ahead – get ahead.

WHY SHOULD WE PLAN UPFRONT?

Planning ahead is very helpful when writing a memoir for several reasons:

- **Organises your thoughts:** It helps you organise your thoughts and ideas, so your story makes sense and flows well.

- **Identifies key moments:** Planning lets you identify the most important moments in your life that you want to share.

- **Saves time:** With a plan, you won't waste time figuring out what to write next. It keeps you on track and focused.

- **Avoids overwhelm:** Writing a memoir can be overwhelming. A plan breaks it into smaller, manageable parts.

- **Ensures completeness:** Planning helps ensure you don't forget any important events or lessons you want to include.

- **Clarifies your message:** It helps you decide what message or theme you want to convey to your readers.

By planning ahead, your memoir will be clearer, more engaging, and easier to write.

WHAT (EXACTLY) IS YOUR MEMOIR ABOUT?

The more we plan upfront now - the easier the writing process will be.

We know the following will be beneficial to be included in our memoir:

- Key moments.
- Key people.
- Key places.
- When we felt vulnerable.
- Lessons we learned.
- Moments of self-reflection.
- Mistakes you made.
- Obstacles you faced and how you overcame them.
- The internal conflict you faced - your inner voice.
- Turning points.
- Theme.

KEY MOMENTS

Key moments are vital when writing a memoir because they:

- Highlight important events: They show the most important events in your life that shaped who you are.

- Make the story interesting: These moments keep the reader interested and make your story exciting.

WHAT (EXACTLY) IS YOUR MEMOIR ABOUT?

Here are examples of key moments within a memoir about climbing Everest:

- Deciding to climb: The moment you decided to climb Everest, explaining why you made this choice. (INCITING EVENT)

- Training: Describing the intense training and preparation needed for the climb.

- First glimpse of Everest: The first time you saw Everest in person, capturing your emotions and thoughts.

- Base Camp arrival: Reaching Base Camp and adjusting to the harsh conditions.

- Challenges faced: Overcoming significant challenges, such as severe weather or health issues like altitude sickness.

- Reaching the summit: The moment you reached the summit, including your feelings and the view from the top.

- Returning safely: The descent and the importance of returning safely, often as challenging as the climb.

KEY PEOPLE

Key people are vital when writing a memoir because they:

- Support your story: They show who helped and supported you on your journey.

- Add depth: They add more detail and richness to your story.

- Show relationships: They help show your important relationships and how they shaped your life.

- Create interest: They make your story more interesting by including different perspectives and interactions.

Including key people makes your memoir more complete and engaging for readers.

WHAT (EXACTLY) IS YOUR MEMOIR ABOUT?

Here are some pretend examples of key people in a memoir about climbing Everest:

- **Experienced Sherpa guide:** The Sherpa who guided you up the mountain and shared his deep knowledge of Everest.

- **Training coach:** Sarah, your fitness coach who helped you prepare physically and mentally for the climb.

- **Climbing partner:** Alex, your close friend and climbing partner, who faced the challenges of the ascent with you.

- **Family member:** Your supportive sister Emma, who encouraged you from home and helped you stay motivated.

- **Expedition leader:** Mr. Johnson, the leader of your climbing expedition, whose leadership was crucial during difficult times.

- **Base Camp doctor:** The doctor who treated your altitude sickness and kept the team healthy.

- **Mentor:** Mr. Thompson, a seasoned climber who inspired you to pursue the Everest dream and gave valuable advice.

These people add depth and dimension to your memoir, making your Everest journey more relatable and engaging.

KEY PLACES

Key places are vital when writing a memoir because they:

- **Set the scene:** They show where important events happened, making the story come alive.

- **Create atmosphere:** They help readers imagine the surroundings and feel the emotions of the place.

- **Show progress:** They mark different stages of your journey, showing how far you've come.

- **Add context:** They give background information that helps readers understand your experiences better.

WHAT (EXACTLY) IS YOUR MEMOIR ABOUT?

Here are some pretend key places for your memoir about climbing Everest:

- Home town: Where your dream of climbing Everest began.

- Training gym: The gym where you trained and prepared for the climb.

- Kathmandu: The city where you started your journey and met your expedition team.

- Base Camp: The Base Camp at the foot of Everest where you acclimated and prepared for the climb.

- Khumbu Icefall: A dangerous section of the climb where you faced great challenges.

- Camp 4: The final camp before the summit push, where you rested and gathered strength.

- Summit: The top of Mount Everest, where you reached your goal and felt immense accomplishment.

- Hospital tent: The place where you recovered from altitude sickness or injuries after the climb.

VULNERABILITIES

Telling about vulnerability in a memoir is vital because it:

- Shows honesty: It shows you are being truthful and real with your readers.

- Builds connection: It helps readers connect with you, as everyone has weaknesses and struggles.

- Creates depth: It adds depth to your story, making it more interesting and relatable.

- Highlights growth: It shows how you overcame challenges, highlighting your personal growth and strength.

WHAT (EXACTLY) IS YOUR MEMOIR ABOUT?

Here are some pretend examples of times somebody may have felt vulnerable during the climb up Mount Everest:

- **Facing altitude sickness:** Feeling weak and dizzy at Base Camp due to altitude sickness, unsure if you could continue.

- **Navigating dangerous icefalls:** Feeling scared and uncertain while crossing the treacherous Khumbu Icefall, with crevasses gaping below.

- **Overcoming fear of heights:** Struggling with fear and doubt while navigating steep and icy slopes near the summit, questioning your ability to keep going.

- **Dealing with isolation:** Feeling lonely and isolated during long stretches of climbing, missing family and friends back home.

- **Enduring harsh weather:** Battling extreme cold and fierce winds during the final push to the summit, wondering if you could endure the conditions.

LEARNING LESSONS

Having lessons learned is vital for a memoir because it:

- **Shares wisdom:** It passes on valuable experiences and insights to readers.

- **Inspires others:** It can inspire others facing similar challenges or goals.

- **Shows growth:** It demonstrates personal growth and development over time.

- **Adds meaning:** It gives purpose to your story, showing how experiences have shaped your life.

WHAT (EXACTLY) IS YOUR MEMOIR ABOUT?

Here are some pretend lessons from climbing Mount Everest:

- Perseverance: I learned that persistence and determination can help overcome even the toughest challenges.

- Teamwork: I realised the importance of working together with others to achieve a common goal, like reaching the summit.

- Resilience: I discovered how to bounce back from setbacks, such as battling altitude sickness or adverse weather conditions.

- Gratitude: I learned to appreciate the small things in life, like warmth, food, and shelter, after experiencing the harsh conditions on the mountain.

- Courage: I found out that facing fears, whether fear of heights or fear of failure, is necessary to achieve great things.

SELF-REFLECTION

Moments of self-reflection in a memoir are vital because they:

- Help understanding: They help you understand yourself better.

- Show growth: They show how you've changed and learned from experiences.

- Add depth: They make your story more thoughtful and meaningful.

- Connect with readers: They allow readers to connect with your thoughts and emotions.

WHAT (EXACTLY) IS YOUR MEMOIR ABOUT?

Here are some pretend examples of moments of <u>self-reflection</u> for the Mount Everest memoir:

- At Base Camp: Reflecting on why you embarked on the Everest journey and what you hoped to achieve.

- Facing challenges: Questioning your own strengths and weaknesses when confronted with difficult terrain or weather conditions.

- After a setback: Thinking about how to bounce back and continue after experiencing a setback, like altitude sickness.

- On the summit: Contemplating the significance of reaching the summit and what it means for your personal goals and growth.

- Returning home: Reflecting on the lessons learned from the climb and how it has changed your perspective on life.

MISTAKES YOU MADE

<u>Mistakes you made</u> are great to include for a memoir because:

- Show humility: They demonstrate that you are honest about your shortcomings and willing to learn from them.

- Teach lessons: They provide opportunities to share valuable lessons learned, helping others avoid similar pitfalls.

- Create drama: They add tension and drama to your story, making it more compelling and engaging for readers.

- Highlight growth: They show how you've grown and developed as a person, overcoming challenges along the way

WHAT (EXACTLY) IS YOUR MEMOIR ABOUT?

Here are some pretend examples of <u>mistakes you could have made</u> during your Mount Everest climb for your pretend memoir:

- Underestimating gear: Bringing inadequate or faulty gear that caused discomfort or slowed progress.

- Ignoring weather warnings: Pressing forward despite clear signs of worsening weather conditions, risking safety.

- Overlooking nutrition: Failing to maintain proper nutrition and hydration, leading to fatigue and decreased performance.

- Poor decision-making: Making hasty decisions under pressure, such as choosing a risky route or ignoring advice from experienced climbers.

- Lack of communication: Not communicating effectively with your team or guides, causing misunderstandings or delays.

OBSTACLES YOU FACED

<u>Obstacles you faced</u> and how you overcame them are gripping for a memoir because:

- Build tension: They create suspense and keep readers interested in how you will overcome each challenge.

- Show resilience: They demonstrate your determination and ability to persevere through difficult situations.

- Inspire readers: They provide inspiration by showing that challenges can be overcome with courage and perseverance.

- Highlight growth: They illustrate personal growth and development as you learn from and conquer obstacles.

WHAT (EXACTLY) IS YOUR MEMOIR ABOUT?

Here are some pretend examples of specific obstacles you faced and how you overcame them during your pretend climb to Mount Everest for your memoir:

- **Altitude sickness:** I struggled with severe headaches and nausea due to altitude sickness at Base Camp. By resting and slowly acclimatising, I was able to continue the climb.

- **Dangerous weather:** During the ascent, a sudden storm hit, bringing heavy snow and strong winds. We found shelter, waited for the storm to pass, and continued once conditions improved.

- **Technical climbing:** Climbing the steep and icy slopes near the summit was challenging. With the help of my guide, I carefully navigated the terrain using proper climbing techniques.

- **Physical exhaustion:** Near the summit push, I felt physically exhausted and doubted my ability to continue. By pacing myself and focusing on small goals, I regained my strength and determination.

- **Equipment failure:** My oxygen tank malfunctioned during the final push to the summit. I quickly switched to a backup tank and continued the climb without further issues.

INNER CONFLICTS

Why are inner conflicts vital for a memoir?

- **Revealing inner turmoil:** They uncover your inner thoughts, doubts, and emotional struggles, adding depth and authenticity to your story.

- **Building suspense:** They create tension and intrigue as readers follow your internal debates and emotional challenges.

- **Highlighting personal growth:** They showcase your journey of self-discovery and development, illustrating how you navigated and resolved internal struggles.

- **Fostering connection:** They foster a deeper connection with readers by showing the human side of your experiences, making your memoir relatable and compelling.

WHAT (EXACTLY) IS YOUR MEMOIR ABOUT?

Here are the pretend examples of <u>internal conflicts</u> you faced during your Mount Everest climb memoir, with some inner dialogue included:

- **Fear vs. determination:** Feeling afraid of the steep, icy slopes near the summit but determined to push forward to achieve your goal.

Inner dialogue: "I'm scared of slipping on this ice, but I've come too far to turn back now. I have to keep going. I can do this."

- **Self-Doubt vs. confidence:** Questioning whether you have the strength and skill to continue the climb versus finding confidence in your preparation and training.

Inner dialogue: "Am I really capable of reaching the summit? Maybe I should listen to my doubts. No, I've trained hard for this. I need to trust myself and keep going."

- **Safety vs. ambition:** Balancing the desire to reach the summit with concerns about safety, especially in challenging weather conditions.

Inner dialogue: "The weather looks risky, but I've dreamt of this moment for years. Is it worth the risk? I need to be smart about this. Safety first, but I can't give up now."

- **Perseverance vs. exhaustion:** Struggling with fatigue and wanting to rest versus pushing yourself to keep moving toward the summit.

Inner dialogue: "I'm so tired, every step feels like a struggle. I want to rest, but I can't stop now. I've trained too hard to quit. Just a little farther, I can make it."

WHAT (EXACTLY) IS YOUR MEMOIR ABOUT?

TURNING POINTS

Turning points are vital in a memoir because:

- **Marking change:** They signify significant moments where your life took a different direction or perspective.

- **Creating interest:** They add excitement and intrigue to your story, keeping readers engaged.

- **Showing growth:** They demonstrate personal growth and development over time.

- **Highlighting impact:** They reveal how events or decisions shaped your life and influenced your journey.

Pretend examples of turning points:

- **Decision to climb:** The moment you committed to the challenging goal of climbing Mount Everest, setting the course for your journey. (This could be the INCITING EVENT - more on that later...)

- **Overcoming fear of heights:** Conquering your fear of heights during training, which boosted your confidence for the climb.

- **Reaching Base Camp:** Arriving at Base Camp and realising the enormity of the challenge ahead, but also feeling excited and determined.

- **Navigating the Khumbu Icefall:** Successfully crossing the treacherous Khumbu Icefall, a daunting obstacle early in the climb.

- **Reaching the summit:** The exhilarating moment when you stood on the summit of Everest, achieving a lifelong dream and feeling immense pride.

WHAT (EXACTLY) IS YOUR MEMOIR ABOUT?

THEME

The theme is important in a memoir because:

- Provides focus: It gives your memoir a central idea or message that ties your experiences together.

- Adds meaning: It gives purpose to your story, showing readers what you want to share or teach through your experiences.

Most common themes for memoirs:

- Resilience and overcoming adversity: Memoirs that focus on triumphing over challenges, obstacles, or personal hardships.

- Self-discovery and personal growth: Stories that explore the journey of self-exploration, change, and transformation.

- Family and relationships: Memoirs that delve into complex family dynamics, relationships, and their impact on personal development.

- Identity and belonging: Themes exploring issues of identity, cultural heritage, and finding one's place in the world.

- Achievement and success: Stories of accomplishing goals, realising dreams, or achieving greatness in a particular field.

- Travel and exploration: Memoirs centred around travel adventures, exploration of new cultures, and the pursuit of experiences.

- Mental health and wellness: Themes dealing with mental health challenges, recovery, and resilience in the face of adversity.

- Social issues and advocacy: Memoirs that advocate for social justice, and equality, or raise awareness about important issues.

WHAT (EXACTLY) IS YOUR MEMOIR ABOUT?

KEY TAKEAWAYS

Engage your reader:

- Include vivid details and personal reflections

- Make your experiences relatable and compelling

Cover important themes:

- Focus on universal themes like love, struggle, and growth

- Ensure your memoir resonates with a wide audience

NOW TURN TO PAGE 140 FOR YOUR END-OF-UNIT ACTIVITY 'YOUR TURN 5' PAGE:

'FILL IN THE OVERVIEW FORM'

YOUR IDEAL READER

YOUR IDEAL READER

SPEAK DIRECTLY TO THE PERSON WHO NEEDS YOUR MEMOIR THE MOST

In this section, you will know EXACTLY who your ideal reader is by filling in your 'Reader Avatar' profile.

WHAT IS A READER AVATAR?

A reader avatar is like an imaginary person that represents the ideal reader of a book or a story.

It helps the writer think about who they are writing for.

- Focus: Writing to an avatar helps the author stay focused on what the reader likes and needs.

- Connection: It helps the author create a stronger connection with the reader by making the story more relatable.

- Consistency: Ensures the story stays consistent and suitable for the target audience.

- Engagement: Makes the story more engaging and interesting for the intended reader.

- Clarity: Helps the author be clear about their writing style and language choice

YOUR IDEAL READER

WHAT DOES A READER AVATAR LOOK LIKE?

Reader avatar for a mountain climbing memoir:

- **Name:** John.

- **Age:** 35.

- **Job:** Engineer.

- **Hobbies:** Hiking, rock climbing, and travelling.

- **Personality:** Adventurous, determined, and enjoys challenges.

- **Goals:** Loves pushing himself to new limits and dreams of climbing the world's tallest mountains.

- **Problems:** Struggles to find time for long adventures due to a busy work schedule, sometimes faces self-doubt about his climbing abilities, and has had a few minor injuries that make him cautious.

- **Reading preferences:** Enjoys true stories about adventure, perseverance, and overcoming obstacles. John is someone who seeks inspiration from real-life experiences and enjoys reading about other climbers' journeys. He is always looking for new challenges and loves learning about different mountain climbing techniques and experiences, despite facing time constraints, self-doubt, and past injuries.

WHY SHOULDN'T I WRITE MY MEMOIR FOR EVERYONE?

- **Too general:** Writing for everyone can make the story too general and less interesting.

- **Less connection:** It might not connect deeply with any specific group of readers.

- **Weak impact:** The memoir might lack the impact and details that make it memorable.

- **Harder to market:** It's harder to market a book without a clear target audience.

- **Less engagement:** Readers may not feel engaged or see themselves in the story.

YOUR IDEAL READER

FOR EXAMPLE

You are a potential customer and you are browsing for a book.

Pretend you can't see the front cover for now.

You read the description and it says:

'This book tells the story of facing difficult situations and is good for anyone who likes reading about real-life events.'

You buy it. You were hoping to read about coping with grief and loss.

But you got a book about the challenges of climbing Everest.

How would you feel as the reader?

BUT IF YOU READ THIS DESCRIPTION...

'Join the exhilarating adventure of a lifetime in "Conquering Everest: A Journey of Triumph and Tribulation."

This gripping memoir takes you through the highs and lows of climbing the world's tallest peak, written for those who seek both inspiration and challenge.

Perfect for adventurous souls who crave real-life stories of courage, Alex's journey will resonate with your passion for climbing and push you to dream bigger. "Conquering Everest" is not just a tale of reaching the summit; it's a testament to the human spirit and the power of never giving up.

Feel the adrenaline, share the fears, and celebrate the victories in this unforgettable story crafted for those who dare to chase their dreams.

Don't miss out on the adventure of a lifetime – get your copy today and start your ascent!'

You'd be more sure of what you were getting!

YOUR IDEAL READER

LOOK AT THE FOLLOWING WORDS THAT WE HIGHLIGHTED

EXHILARATING ADVENTURE	CLIMBING THE WORLD'S TALLEST PEAK	NEVER GIVING UP
ADVENTUROUS SOULS	COURAGE	ADRENALINE

'Join the exhilarating adventure of a lifetime in "Conquering Everest: A Journey of Triumph and Tribulation."

This gripping memoir takes you through the highs and lows of climbing the world's tallest peak, written for those who seek both inspiration and challenge.

Perfect for adventurous souls who crave real-life stories of courage. Alex's journey will resonate with your passion for climbing and push you to dream bigger. "Conquering Everest" is not just a tale of reaching the summit; it's a testament to the human spirit and the power of never giving up.

Feel the adrenaline, share the fears, and celebrate the victories in this unforgettable story crafted for those who dare to chase their dreams.

Don't miss out on the adventure of a lifetime – get your copy today and start your ascent!'

It spells out exactly who is it for and what's inside. There is no confusion as to what you will get.

Confused buyers = BAD.

Our reader knows EXACTLY what it's about. They are less likely to return it/ask for a refund/give a bad review. They will be inspired by it. They can see 'themselves' in the book description.

Plus, YOU will know exactly who you are writing for and will make sure you include the important parts in your memoir.

If you ever wanted to market your memoir, you will get a match with your ideal reader more easily!

Match with reader = SALES!

YOUR IDEAL READER

HOW DO I KNOW THE ANSWERS TO THE 'READER AVATAR' QUESTIONS?

Your ideal reader is...

YOU!

Yes.

It doesn't get any more complicated than that.

You are your reader avatar.

Why?

Because you as you, went through the entire experience with your thoughts, feelings and problems.

So you are the expert and you would be the ideal reader.

So if at the time of the event you were in your 20s.

Your ideal avatar would/could be in their 20s.

If you had just lost your job, your ideal reader may have just lost their job, or looking for a job etc.

So your avatar could be:

'Adult in their 20s who is facing the prospect of losing their job...'

They will feel like you are speaking DIRECTLY to them.

And if you speak directly to them, they are more likely to identify with everything you say and will trust you will help them.

YOUR IDEAL READER

KEY TAKEAWAYS

- Targeted content:

    - Write stories and details that will interest your specific reader.
    - Make sure your memoir speaks directly to their preferences and interests.

- Relevant themes:

    - Focus on themes and experiences your reader can relate to.
    - Address their needs and curiosities to keep them engaged.

- Personal connection:

    - Use language and tone that resonate with your reader.
    - Create a memoir that feels personal and meaningful to them.

NOW TURN TO PAGE 144 FOR YOUR END-OF-UNIT ACTIVITY 'YOUR TURN 6' PAGE:

'YOUR READER AVATAR'

THE INCITING EVENT

THE INCITING EVENT

THE EVENT THAT STARTED EVERYTHING

In this section, you will create a gripping start to your memoir using our '3 Part Backwards Building Block' method that ensures you don't waffle, wander and lose your reader but instead –

Start with a BANG!

WHAT IS AN INCITING EVENT?

An inciting event is the big moment in your story that changed everything.

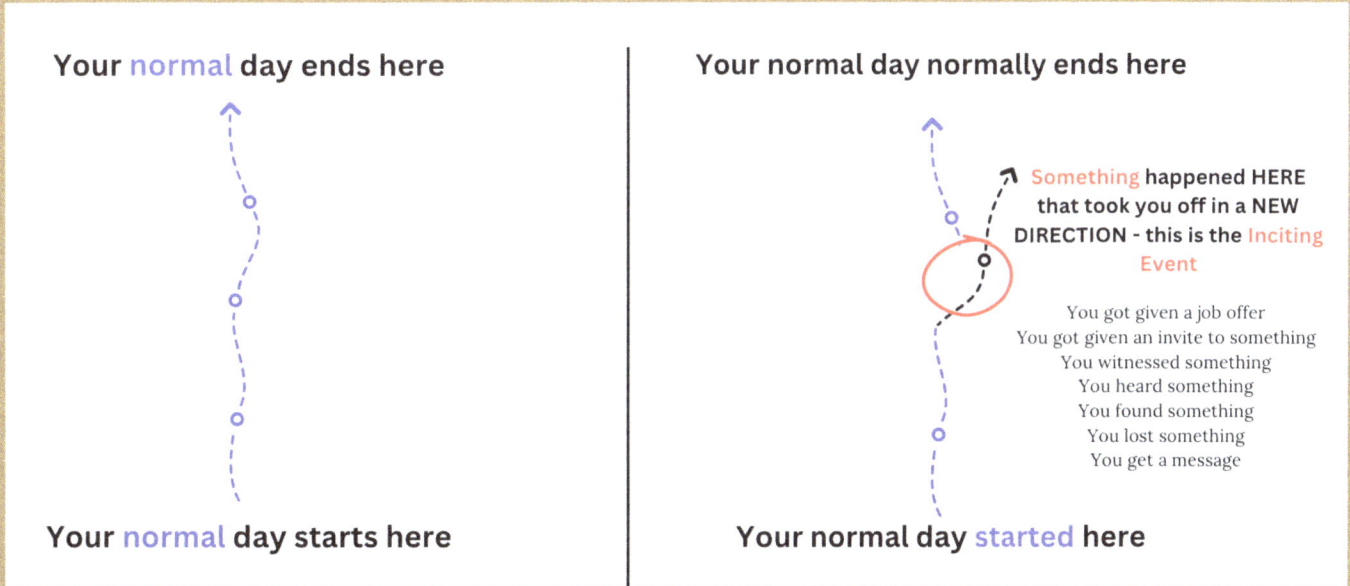

EXAMPLES OF INCITING EVENTS IN MOVIES –

- **Harry Potter:** When Harry gets his letter from Hogwarts, his life changes forever. He finds out he is a wizard!

- **The Lion King:** When Simba's father, Mufasa, dies, Simba's life changes. He has to leave home and find his way back.

- **Finding Nemo:** When Nemo gets captured by divers, Marlin, his father, starts his big journey to find him.

The words in GREEN are the Inciting Event – the thing/the moment everything changed.

THE INCITING EVENT

WHY DO WE HAVE INCITING EVENTS IN MEMOIRS?

We have Inciting Events in memoirs to make the story exciting and interesting.

These events start the main action and grab the reader's attention.

They show what changes the author's life and set the stage for the rest of the story.

This helps readers understand why the story is important and keeps them wanting to read more.

LET'S TALK ABOUT REAL LIFE...

Think back to when your life drastically changed direction – write it down.

You will be able to clearly see your Inciting Event – the event that changed everything.

Eg: I was on watch, it was 2 am and I only had two hours to go until I could get back into my bed all warm and cosy. I was struggling to keep my eyes open, then I got a 'beep'. It was a message from my mate at the barracks he said 'Look at the news'. I put the news on and saw that a war had kicked off. Once I got off watch, I got notified that I was going to war the next day. This was it.

My Inciting Event is: 'I got notified I was going to war the next day.'

THE INCITING EVENT

THE 'HOOKY' QUESTION

Hooks make the reader curious about what will happen next.

A good hook can be surprising, exciting, or intriguing, making the reader want to find out more and keep turning the pages.

That's what we want.

You can make a good hook by asking a question that gets the reader to think.

You want to ask a 'will they or won't they question' – these work well.

LET'S SEE THIS IN ACTION...

We have our Inciting Event: Now to answer some questions about it.

- What did we feel about it?

- What did we think the biggest obstacle would be when we found out about the Inciting Event?

- Why do we have this? We want our readers to know what we have to overcome and wonder if we do overcome it, and if so, how did we do that?

THE INCITING EVENT

EXAMPLE

- Write your Inciting Event line here:

    I got notified I was going to war the next day.

- Write how you felt about it in 1-3 words:

    Shocked, scared and overwhelmed.

- What main obstacle would you face?

    Being ready for war.

- Now write that obstacle as a question:

    Was I ready to fight in a war zone?

NOW WE PUT IT IN A SENTENCE

(Inciting Event) 'I got notified I was going to war the next day. I felt shocked, scared and overwhelmed.
(Hooky question) Was I really ready to fight in a war-zone?'

THE INCITING EVENT

THE 'MOMENTS BEFORE' BIT

This is the part YOU HAVE ALREADY written, but we will just make it more detailed (but not too fluffy).

Our pretend example NOW INCLUDES A 'MOMENTS BEFORE':

'I was on watch, it was 2 am and I only had two hours to go until I could get back into my bed all warm and cosy. I was struggling to keep my eyes open, then I got a 'beep'. It was a message from my mate at the barracks he said 'Look at the news'. I put the news on and saw that a war had kicked off. Once I got off watch, I got notified that I was going to war the next day. This was it.' (INCITING EVENT)

Let's add some small details to make it more immersive: (Tip: Use the 5 senses)

It may look something like this:

'I was on watch, it was 2 am, and I only had two hours to go until I could get back into my warm, cosy bed.

The cold night air nipped at my face, and the distant hum of the barracks was the only sound breaking the silence.

The smell of damp grass and the metallic scent of my gear filled the air. I was struggling to keep my eyes open, my hands wrapped tightly around a steaming cup of tea, the warmth spreading through my fingers.

Then I got a 'beep'. It was a message from my mate at the barracks: 'Look at the news.' My heart pounded as I switched on the small radio. The news blared, and I saw that a war had kicked off. The reality hit me like a punch in the gut.

THE INCITING EVENT

THE 'MOMENTS BEFORE' BIT

Let's put the whole thing together in the CORRECT order:

(Moments before the Inciting Event)
I was on watch, it was 2 am, and I only had two hours to go until I could get back into my warm, cosy bed.

The cold night air nipped at my face, and the distant hum of the barracks was the only sound breaking the silence.

The smell of damp grass and the metallic scent of my gear filled the air. I was struggling to keep my eyes open, my hands wrapped tightly around a steaming cup of tea, the warmth spreading through my fingers.

Then I got a 'beep'. It was a message from my mate at the barracks: 'Look at the news.' My heart pounded as I switched on the small radio. The news blared, and I saw that a war had kicked off. The reality hit me like a punch in the gut.

(Inciting Event) I got notified I was going to war the next day. I felt shocked, scared and overwhelmed.

(Hooky question) Was I really ready to fight in a war-zone?'

You have now created a gripping start to your memoir!

THE INCITING EVENT

KEY TAKEAWAYS

- **Inciting Events:** They start the main action of the story and make readers want to know what happens next.

- **Hooky questions:** These grab the reader's attention and make them curious, encouraging them to keep reading.

- **Setting the scene:** Describing the scene before the inciting event helps readers picture where the story takes place and feel more connected to it

WHAT WE HAVE NOW

The Structure of Your Memoir
'The Building Blocks'

- Title
- Sub-Title
- Wallop Scene
- Childhood
- Everyday life before
- Inciting Event ✓
- Chapters
- Conclusion

NOW TURN TO <u>PAGES 146-152</u> FOR YOUR END-OF-UNIT ACTIVITIES:

YOUR TURN 7: 'YOUR INCITING EVENT'
YOUR TURN 8: 'YOUR HOOKY QUESTION'
YOUR TURN 9: YOUR 'MOMENTS BEFORE'
YOUR TURN 10: 'PUTTING THEM ALL TOGETHER'

Everyday Life 2-3 Years Before the Inciting Event

EVERYDAY LIFE 2-3 YEARS BEFORE THE INCITING EVENT

In this section, you will easily show the start of your epic transformation by giving your readers a glimpse into your EVERYDAY life before it changed. (Around 2-3 years BEFORE the 'Inciting Event')

WHY IS SHOWING THE VERY START OF YOUR TRANSFORMATION IMPORTANT IN YOUR MEMOIR?

The start of a transformation shows:

- Initial challenges: Illustrates the first obstacles faced, making the journey realistic.

- Motivation: Reveals what drives the person to change, adding purpose to their actions.

- Foundation: Sets the stage for future growth and development, making the transformation impactful.

Basically, we get to see YOU before the BIG CHANGE happened (the Inciting Event)

When you complete your journey, we have something (context) to compare it to.

- We see your before and after.

- Your start and your end.

- Your transformation.

EVERYDAY LIFE 2-3 YEARS BEFORE THE INCITING EVENT

EVERYDAY LIFE BEFORE YOUR INCITING EVENT

Knowing about someone's life before the Inciting Event is beneficial because it:

- **Provides context:** Helps us understand their normal daily routine and lifestyle.

- **Highlights changes:** Shows how the journey or challenges will disrupt their usual life.

- **Builds connection:** Makes it easier to relate to them and their experiences

HOW EXACTLY DO WE DO THIS?

We just need to know what your EVERYDAY life was like <u>BEFORE</u> you knew about the Inciting Event.

- What would your daily routine look like?

- What were your priorities in life?

- What were your goals and dreams?

- Where were you based?

EVERYDAY LIFE 2-3 YEARS BEFORE THE INCITING EVENT

LET'S LOOK AT AN EXAMPLE FOR OUR EVEREST CLIMB

Let's pretend we are filling out the answers for 'John' our Everest climber BEFORE he got the opportunity to climb Everest.

Daily routine: Describe your typical day. What did you do? Who did you spend time with? Where did you go?

Emotions: How did you feel during this time? Were you happy, content, bored, or worried about something?

Important relationships: Who were the key people in your life? Family, friends, colleagues?

Personal goals: What were your goals or dreams before the event? What were you working towards or hoping for?

Setting: Describe the places that were important to you. Your home, workplace, favourite hangout spots

JOHN'S EXAMPLE

Daily routine: John's typical day started early in the morning. He would wake up, have a quick breakfast, and then head to the warehouse in Birmingham where he worked. His job involved heavy lifting, sorting boxes, and long hours of repetitive tasks. After work, he would go home, watch TV, and then go to bed, ready to repeat the cycle the next day.

Emotions: John felt trapped and bored. His job brought him no joy, and he often felt a sense of frustration and longing for something more fulfilling. There were days when he felt utterly exhausted, both physically and emotionally.

Important relationships: John's key relationships were with his family and a few close friends. His parents lived nearby, and he would visit them occasionally. He had a small circle of friends he met up with sometimes, but they all seemed busy with their own lives.

EVERYDAY LIFE 2-3 YEARS BEFORE THE INCITING EVENT

Personal goals: Before the event, John's main goal was simply to get through each day. He had dreams of finding a more satisfying job and perhaps travelling, but these felt distant and unreachable given his current situation.

Setting: The important places in John's life included his small flat in Birmingham, which was modest and often felt lonely. The warehouse was a large, cold building filled with noise and activity but void of personal meaning. Occasionally, he would visit a local pub with his friends, which provided a brief escape from his mundane routine.

LET'S PUT IT ALL TOGETHER TO MAKE IT A READABLE PARAGRAPH

My typical day started early in the morning. I would wake up, have a quick breakfast, and then head to the warehouse in Birmingham where I worked. My job involved heavy lifting, sorting boxes, and long hours of repetitive tasks. After work, I would go home, watch TV, and then go to bed, ready to repeat the cycle the next day.

I felt trapped and bored. My job brought me no joy, and I often felt a sense of frustration and longing for something more fulfilling. There were days when I felt utterly exhausted, both physically and emotionally.

My key relationships were with my family and a few close friends. My parents lived nearby, and I would visit them occasionally. I had a small circle of friends I met up with sometimes, but they all seemed busy with their own lives. Before the event, my main goal was simply to get through each day. I had dreams of finding a more satisfying job and perhaps travelling, but these felt distant and unreachable given my current situation.

The important places in my life included my small flat in Birmingham, which was modest and often felt lonely. The warehouse was a large, cold building filled with noise and activity but void of personal meaning. Occasionally, I would visit a local pub with my friends, which provided a brief escape from my mundane routine.

EVERYDAY LIFE 2-3 YEARS BEFORE THE INCITING EVENT

Can you imagine the change (transformation) from THIS guy to the guy who stands on top of Mount Everest?

If we just focused on the success (the end), we wouldn't be able to appreciate the journey that John had to experience to achieve it.

WHAT TO LEAVE OUT

- Too many details: Avoid including every single detail of your daily life. Focus on what gives a clear picture.

- Unrelated events: Skip events or stories that do not connect to or set up the Inciting Event.

- Long descriptions: Keep descriptions brief and to the point. Only add details that enhance the reader's understanding.

KEY TAKEAWAYS

- Shows growth: Helps readers see how much the person has changed.

- Builds connection: Makes it easier to relate to the person's struggles and achievements.

- Highlights challenges: Emphasises how tough the journey was compared to their old life.

EVERYDAY LIFE 2-3 YEARS BEFORE THE INCITING EVENT

WHAT WE HAVE NOW

The Structure of Your Memoir
'The Building Blocks'

- Title
- Sub-Title
- Wallop Scene
- Childhood
- Everyday life before ✓
- Inciting Event ✓
- Chapters
- Conclusion

NOW TURN TO **PAGE 154** FOR YOUR END-OF-UNIT ACTIVITY 'YOUR TURN 11' PAGE:

'EVERYDAY LIFE BEFORE THE INCITING EVENT'

YOUR CHILDHOOD

YOUR CHILDHOOD

YOUR CHILDHOOD UP UNTIL THE 'EVERYDAY LIFE BEFORE' PART

In this section, you will share the YOU before life happened by filling in the 'Childhood Questionnaire' so your readers can really get to know you.

Why does knowing about your childhood (briefly) help your readers?

Knowing about your childhood briefly helps with context in a memoir because it:

- Sets the scene: Provides background on your early experiences.

- Explains influences: Shows what shaped your beliefs and values.

- Builds understanding: Helps readers understand your journey and growth.

But how much childhood should I include?

In a memoir, childhood should be included enough to provide context and understanding of significant influences and experiences that shaped the person's later life.

However, the focus should primarily be on specific events, themes, or periods that relate directly to the main story or central theme of the memoir.

This approach ensures that the memoir remains focused and thematic, rather than becoming a comprehensive autobiography covering every aspect of the author's life.

YOUR CHILDHOOD

EXAMPLE

Our pretend guy 'John' - the Everest climber.

- When and where were you born?

I was born on May 15, 1985, in Birmingham, UK.

- What are your earliest memories?

My earliest memory is playing in the backyard with his older sister and their dog.

- Who were the key people in your early life (family, caregivers, friends)?

Key people included my parents, Sarah and Michael, my older sister Emma, and my best friend from primary school, Tom.

- What was your family dynamic like (parents' occupations, siblings, family traditions)?

My father worked as a mechanic, and my mother was a nurse. They emphasised family dinners together every evening and outings on weekends.

- Where did you grow up (describe your hometown or neighbourhood)?

I grew up in a modest neighbourhood in Birmingham, surrounded by rows of terraced houses and a local park where he played football with friends.

YOUR CHILDHOOD

EXAMPLE

Our pretend guy 'John' - the Everest climber.

- What schools did you attend? Any memorable teachers or classmates?

I attended St. Mary's Primary School and later Birmingham Secondary School. My favourite teacher was Mr. Johnson, who encouraged his interest in science.

- What were your favourite childhood activities or hobbies?

I enjoyed playing football with friends, reading adventure books, and tinkering with old radios and gadgets.

- Did you have any significant childhood challenges or obstacles?

I struggled with shyness and making new friends when I moved to a new school in Year 7.

- What was your wildest dream?

As a child, my wildest dream was to build a robot that could explore outer space—a dream fueled by my love for science fiction and my fascination with how things work.

YOUR CHILDHOOD

EXAMPLE

Let's tweak it a bit and put it into a readable paragraph to give our readers some context about John's upbringing... (don't forget to use the 5 senses here)

I lived my early years in Birmingham, born on a spring day in 1985. Some of my earliest memories are of playing in our backyard with my older sister Emma and our loyal dog.

My parents, Sarah and Michael, shaped my upbringing; Dad was a hardworking mechanic, while Mum, a nurse, always made sure we gathered for family dinners every night.

Our neighbourhood was filled with rows of terraced houses and a nearby park where I spent endless afternoons playing football with friends. At St. Mary's Primary School and later Birmingham Secondary School, I thrived under the guidance of Mr. Johnson, a teacher who nurtured my curiosity for science.

Despite moving schools in Year 7, my love for tinkering with gadgets and reading adventure books remained constant. Family gatherings at my grandparents' house were always lively affairs during holidays, filled with laughter and good food.

Winning a science fair in Year 6 was a pivotal moment that sparked my dream of becoming an engineer. Growing up, my parents instilled in me the values of hard work, honesty, and respect for others, while occasional visits to church provided a sense of community.

Cannon Hill Park and the Birmingham Museum and Art Gallery were my favourite spots to explore on weekends, adding a touch of wonder to my childhood days in Birmingham. As a child, my wildest dream was to build a robot that could explore outer space—a dream fueled by my love for science fiction and my fascination with how things work.

YOUR CHILDHOOD

KEY TAKEAWAYS

Knowing about some of your childhood is important in a memoir as the reader gets to:

- Understand your values.

- Understand where it all began.

- Understand early struggles you may have had to face - hence making your journey/achievement more poignant.

WHAT WE HAVE NOW

The Structure of Your Memoir
'The Building Blocks'

- Title
- Sub-Title
- Wallop Scene
- Childhood ✓
- Everyday life before ✓
- Inciting Event ✓
- Chapters
- Conclusion

NOW TURN TO PAGE 158 FOR YOUR END-OF-UNIT ACTIVITY 'YOUR TURN 12' PAGE:

'YOUR CHILDHOOD'

THE 12 STEPS

THE 12 STEPS

THE BODY OF YOUR MEMOIR: FROM START TO FINISH

In this section, you will feel confident in your planning as you see your whole story on a page by using our 12 Steps Process.

Each step is a chapter!

The Structure of Your Memoir
'The Building Blocks'

- Title
- Sub-Title
- Wallop Scene
- Childhood
- Everyday life before
- Inciting Event
- Chapters
- Conclusion

THE 12 STEPS

WHY PLAN UPFRONT?

Planning your memoir story upfront is beneficial because it helps you stay organised, ensures your story flows well, and makes it easier to include important details and events.

You can 'see' your story easier.

You can tell how balanced it is.

HOW DO WE DO THIS?

- We literally divide the main part of our story into 12 parts.

- Each part is a chapter in your story.

- Each part is an important moment in the process from our start to finish.

LET'S SEE IT ACTION...

Let's pretend we are writing our memoir on climbing Mount Everest.

- Brainstorm ALL the moments you can think of that took place between the start and finish.

- Then put those into chronological order.

- Make sure they are around 12 steps approx – ONLY include the most important/dramatic steps – leave the rest.

- These are your chapters.

THE 12 STEPS

EXAMPLE FOR MOUNT EVEREST – HERE IT IS

Step 1 – Saying yes to climbing it and getting ready (This is what happened after the INCITING EVENT).

Step 2 – Finding the team.

Step 3 – Getting gear and supplies.

Step 4 – Travelling to Base Camp.

Step 5 – Adjusting at Base Camp.

Step 6 – Starting the climb.

Step 7 – Crossing the Khumbu Icefall.

Step 8 – Climbing the Lhotse Face.

Step 9 – Reaching the South Col.

Step 10 – Summit climb.

Step 11 – Reaching the summit.

Step 12 – Safe return and going home.

THE 12 STEPS
KEY TAKEAWAYS

Planning your chapters upfront:

- Helps you stay organised.

- Helps you see your whole memoir on a page.

- Ensures your story flows well.

WHAT WE HAVE NOW
The Structure of Your Memoir
'The Building Blocks'

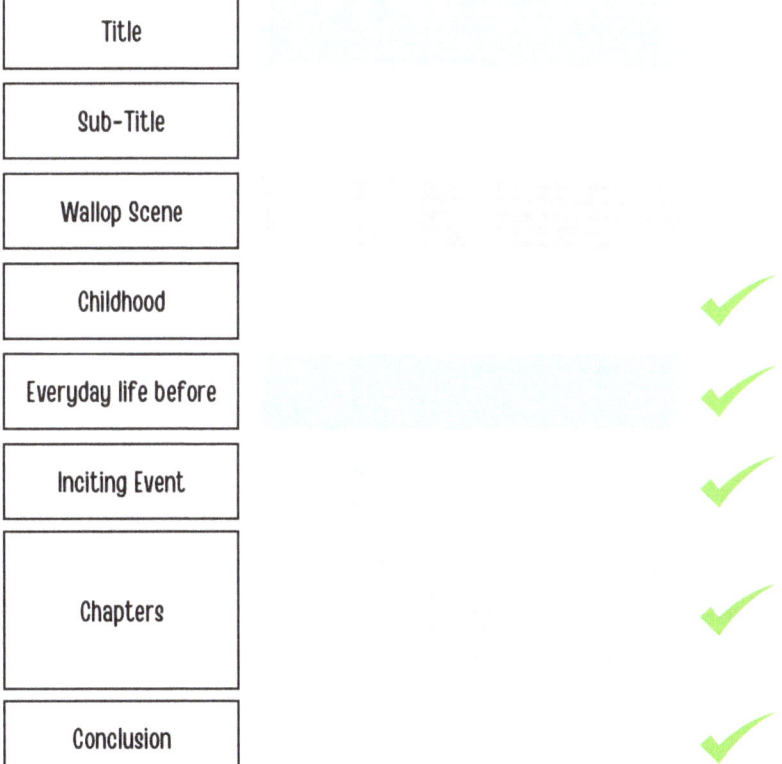

- Title
- Sub-Title
- Wallop Scene
- Childhood ✓
- Everyday life before ✓
- Inciting Event ✓
- Chapters ✓
- Conclusion ✓

NOW TURN TO PAGE 162 FOR YOUR END-OF-UNIT ACTIVITY 'YOUR TURN 13' PAGE:

'YOUR 12 STEPS'

FIRST, NEXT AND LAST...

FIRST, NEXT AND LAST...

CONTENT FOR EACH CHAPTER

In this section, you will organise the content *within* each chapter (step) into chronological order using our 'First, next and last' process that ensures you don't waffle or wander off course. You will feel confident as it all starts coming together nicely.

WHAT IS THE FIRST, NEXT AND LAST PROCESS?

We discovered this method whilst researching parts for this course and it made sense. To be honest, I (Vicky) wished I had used it for my memoir.

First, next and last is very simple.

Within each chapter (step), you divide it into 3 smaller parts.

- What happened first?
- What happened next?
- Then what happened last?

BENEFITS TO YOU BY DOING THIS METHOD

Clear progression: Ensure each part (First, Next, Last) logically follows from the previous one, creating a smooth flow and maintaining the reader's interest.

Focused details: Keep each section concise and focused on specific events or actions, helping to build a coherent narrative and avoid confusion.

Natural transitions: Use transitional phrases or sentences to link each part seamlessly, guiding the reader through the chapter without abrupt jumps.

FIRST, NEXT AND LAST...

LET'S SEE IT IN ACTION WITH OUR EVEREST EXAMPLE

So, within each step/chapter, write what happened exactly and in what order (we will go into more detail later don't worry, we need the scene headings first - see below)

Step 1 - Saying yes to the climb and getting ready

FIRST: Telling my family.

NEXT: Posting on social media.

LAST: Thinking what I might need.

Step 1 - Saying yes and getting ready (This is what happened after the INCITING EVENT).

Step 2 - Finding the team.

Step 3 - Getting gear and supplies.

Step 4 - Travelling to Base Camp.

Step 5 - Adjusting at Base Camp.

Step 6 - Starting the climb.

Step 7 - Crossing the Khumbu Icefall.

Step 8 - Climbing the Lhotse Face.

Step 9 - Reaching the South Col.

Step 10 - Summit climb.

Step 11 - Reaching the summit.

Step 12 - Safe return and going home.

FIRST, NEXT AND LAST...

LET'S SEE IT IN ACTION WITH OUR EVEREST EXAMPLE

It may look like this later:

Step 1 (chapter 1) - Saying yes and getting ready

FIRST: Telling my family.

- Sharing the news with my loved ones and discussing the challenges ahead.

NEXT: Posting on social media.

- Announcing my decision online, receiving support, and answering questions from friends and followers.

LAST: Thinking what I might need.

- Making a preliminary list of gear, training requirements, and other preparations.

So, within each step/chapter, write what happened exactly and in what order (we will go into more detail later don't worry, we need the scene headings first - see below)

Step 2 (chapter 2) - Finding the team

FIRST: Researching climbing groups.

NEXT: Contacting potential teammates.

LAST: Meeting the team.

Step 1 - Saying yes and getting ready (This is what happened after the INCITING EVENT).
Step 2 - Finding the team.
Step 3 - Getting gear and supplies.
Step 4 - Travelling to Base Camp.
Step 5 - Adjusting at Base Camp.
Step 6 - Starting the climb.
Step 7 - Crossing the Khumbu Icefall.
Step 8 - Climbing the Lhotse Face.
Step 9 - Reaching the South Col.
Step 10 - Summit climb.
Step 11 - Reaching the summit.
Step 12 - Safe return and going home.

FIRST, NEXT AND LAST...

Remember – You have the answers to all of these things.

If at first you have to brainstorm the things that happened, then pick the most important 3 things and put THEM in chronological order.

FIRST
NEXT
LAST

KEY TAKEAWAYS

- **Logical flow:** Each part should follow logically to maintain smooth progression.

- **Concise focus:** Keep sections concise and event - focused for clarity.

- **Seamless transitions:** Use transitions to link parts naturally.

NOW TURN TO **PAGE 165** FOR YOUR END-OF-UNIT ACTIVITY 'YOUR TURN 14' PAGE:

'FIRST, NEXT AND LAST...'

YOUR TITLE AND SUB-TITLE

YOUR TITLE AND SUBTITLE

In this section, you will create a scroll-stopping title and sub-title with ease using our 'Title Generating Framework'

WHY ARE HOOKY TITLES AND SUB-TITLES VITAL?

Hooky titles and subtitles are vital for a memoir, especially when the author may not be well-known, for several key reasons:

- **Attracts reader's attention:** A hooky title grabs the reader's attention immediately, drawing them into the memoir even if they are unfamiliar with the author. This is crucial in a competitive market where readers have numerous choices.

- **Communicates key themes quickly:** Keywords in the title and subtitle convey the central themes and emotional core of the memoir. This helps potential readers quickly understand what the book is about and whether it aligns with their interests.

- **Enhances discoverability:** Memorable and descriptive titles with strong keywords improve the chances of the memoir being discovered through online searches or browsing in bookstores. They make it easier for readers to find and remember the book among other options.

- **Generates curiosity and buzz:** Hooky titles and subtitles generate curiosity and intrigue, prompting readers to want to learn more about the story behind the captivating title. This can lead to word-of-mouth recommendations and increased interest in the memoir.

- **Establishes the author's voice and brand:** For lesser-known authors, a hooky title and subtitle can help establish their unique voice and brand in the memoir genre, making them stand out and memorable to readers.

YOUR TITLE AND SUBTITLE

WHAT NOT TO DO

Example 1: "My Journey"

Issue: This title is extremely vague and does not provide any indication of what the memoir is about. It lacks specificity and fails to capture the reader's interest or convey the unique aspects of the story.

Example 2: "Life Lessons"

Issue: While this title suggests the memoir involves lessons learned, it is overly generic and could apply to countless books. It does not distinguish the memoir from others or give readers a compelling reason to choose it over alternative titles.

Using Clichés:

Example 1: "Against All Odds"

Issue: This phrase is a common cliché often used to describe stories of overcoming challenges. It lacks originality and may give the impression that the memoir follows a predictable narrative without offering fresh insights or perspectives.

Example 2: "Through the Darkness"

Issue: Similar to the previous example, "Through the Darkness" is a clichéd metaphor often used to symbolise struggles and adversity.

It does not provide specific details about the memoir's content or distinguish it from other memoirs with similar themes.

HOW YOU WILL DO IT?

By using a framework that will help you construct a great title and sub-title - this is on YOUR TURN 15 page 170.

YOUR TITLE AND SUBTITLE

KEY TAKEAWAYS

- **Captures attention:** A strong title and subtitle immediately grab the reader's interest, encouraging them to pick up the memoir and delve into the story.

- **Sets expectations:** They provide clarity about the themes, emotions, and experiences explored in the memoir, guiding readers on what to expect and enticing them with promises of what they will discover.

- **Memorable impression:** A well-crafted title and subtitle leave a lasting impression, making it easier for readers to remember and recommend the memoir to others, thus increasing its impact and reach.

WHAT WE HAVE NOW

The Structure of Your Memoir

'The Building Blocks'

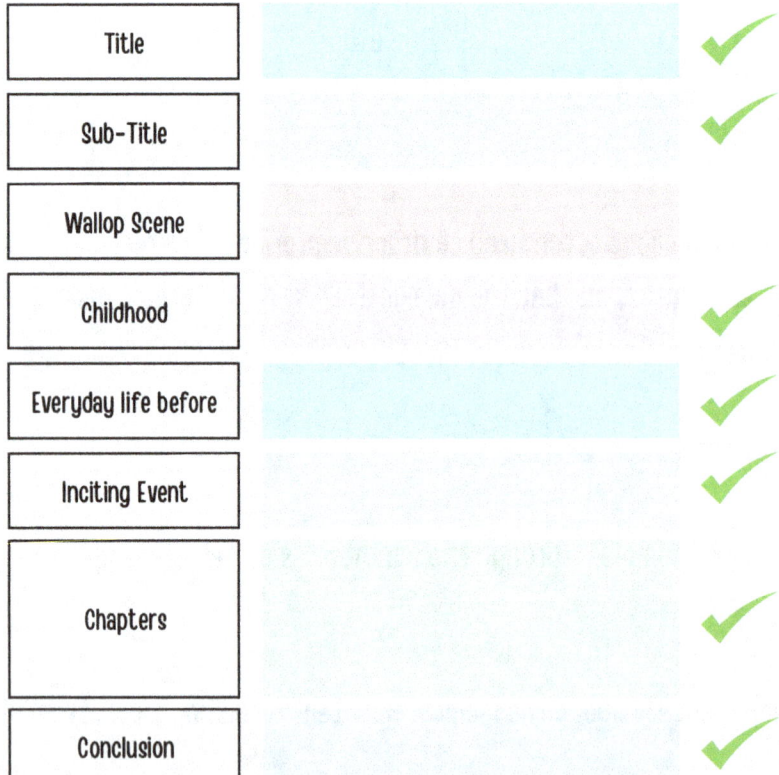

NOW TURN TO PAGE 170 FOR YOUR END-OF-UNIT ACTIVITY 'YOUR TURN 15' PAGE:

'YOUR TITLE AND SUBTITLE'

YOUR LOGLINE

YOUR LOGLINE

In this section, you will write a compelling mini sales pitch using our 'Logline Framework' that ensures your memoir comes alive!

WHAT IS A LOGLINE?

A logline is a brief summary that captures the essence of a story.

It typically includes information about the main character, their goals or challenges, the setting, and why the story is compelling or important.

It's like a snapshot that gives you a quick idea of what the story is about.

WHERE/WHEN/WHY ARE LOGLINES USED?

Pitching to publishers: Authors use loglines when pitching their manuscripts to literary agents and publishers. A well-crafted logline quickly communicates the essence of the memoir, helping to generate interest and secure representation or publication.

Book descriptions and blurbs: Publishers use loglines in book descriptions and blurbs on websites, catalogues, and promotional materials. A compelling logline grabs potential readers' attention and gives them a clear idea of what the memoir is about, encouraging them to pick up the book.

Marketing and promotion: Authors and publishers use loglines in marketing campaigns, including social media posts, press releases, and advertisements. A strong logline helps create buzz and attract readers by highlighting the unique aspects and emotional core of the memoir.

Reader engagement: Readers encounter loglines when browsing online bookstores or libraries. A well-crafted logline helps readers quickly assess whether a memoir aligns with their interests and motivations for reading, influencing their decision to explore further or make a purchase.

YOUR LOGLINE

EXAMPLE LOGLINES FOR MEMOIRS

John, an ambitious mountaineer, faces crippling self-doubt and physical challenges while climbing the treacherous slopes of Mount Everest, and must conquer his inner fears to prove his worth and fulfill his lifelong dream of reaching the summit.

Lucy, a determined entrepreneur, navigates the cutthroat world of corporate America, and must overcome betrayal and self-doubt to achieve her dream of creating a successful business empire and empowering women in leadership roles.

David, a troubled war veteran, confronts the harsh realities of survival and his inner demons in the rugged wilderness of Alaska, and must find redemption and peace to reconcile with his past and reconnect with his family.

Ella, an adventurous soul, faces the challenge of navigating cultural barriers and self-doubt in the bustling streets of Tokyo, and must achieve the clarity needed to pursue her true passions to find fulfillment.

HOW DO WE CREATE A LOGLINE?

Use a very basic framework

[Protagonist's Name], a [brief description of protagonist], faces [conflict], in [location or setting], and must [achieve/overcome] to [stakes or consequences].

The protagonist is the main character = YOU

YOUR LOGLINE

KEY TAKEAWAYS

- **Clarity:** Loglines quickly explain what a memoir is about.

- **Interest:** They make people curious to read more.

- **Marketing:** Loglines help sell memoirs to readers and publishers.

NOW TURN TO **PAGE 177** FOR YOUR END-OF-UNIT ACTIVITY 'YOUR TURN 16' PAGE:

'YOUR LOGLINE'

WRITING YOUR MEMOIR OUTLINE

WRITING YOUR MEMOIR OUTLINE

In this section, you will use the 12 Step Outline to create an extended version of your memoir plan with ease. It will ensure you'll later write with flow, banishing writer's block and only keeping in what's relevant which will keep your readers engaged at every point in your story.

WHY DO WE USE A DETAILED OUTLINE?

- **Organises ideas:** A detailed outline helps you arrange your thoughts and memories in a clear order, making it easier to write your story.

- **Maintains focus:** It keeps you on track, ensuring you don't stray from the main events and themes of your memoir.

- **Improves flow:** Outlining helps you create a smooth narrative flow, making your story more engaging and easier to follow.

- **Saves time:** By planning ahead, you reduce the time spent figuring out what to write next, allowing for more efficient writing sessions.

- **Highlights gaps:** An outline can reveal any missing details or gaps in your story, giving you the chance to fill them in before you start writing.

WRITING YOUR MEMOIR OUTLINE

WHY DO WE USE A DETAILED OUTLINE?

It makes sure you write about the MAIN thing that happened in that scene:

This is literally the point of that particular scene.

- The 5 senses (see, hear, touch, taste and smell): This will bring your scenes alive and make them much more immersive.

- Characters involved: Who was involved in this scene, this will help you think of conversations etc.

- Action: What actually took place, and why? How?

- Dialogue: This makes your memoir a more human experience – like we are overhearing conversations as if we are there.

- Conflict: Something goes wrong, or something wasn't as easy as we thought it would be – creates tension.

- Emotions: What were you feeling 'at the time' – this pulls us into your world which means we will feel empathy.

- Internal thoughts: The dialogue nobody else hears. This makes for compelling storytelling as we get to hear how you REALLY felt and why.

- Resolution: How did that particular scene end and why? Were you happy with it? Did you have worries going forward?

- Lessons learned: This is huge for a memoir – what mistakes did you make? What would you have done differently and why? What prevented you from doing certain things that you would change today?

WRITING YOUR MEMOIR OUTLINE

For every scene, if we include answers from those prompts, our memoir will be filled with gripping scenes, advice, action and vulnerability. Which automatically makes for a gripping memoir!

KEY TAKEAWAYS

- **Brings scenes to life:** Including dialogue and action makes your scenes more vivid and engaging, helping readers imagine the events as if they were there.

- **Deepens understanding:** Sharing internal thoughts and lessons learned allows readers to connect with your experiences and understand your personal growth.

- **Introduces key people:** Describing the characters involved helps readers get to know the important people in your life and their impact on your story.

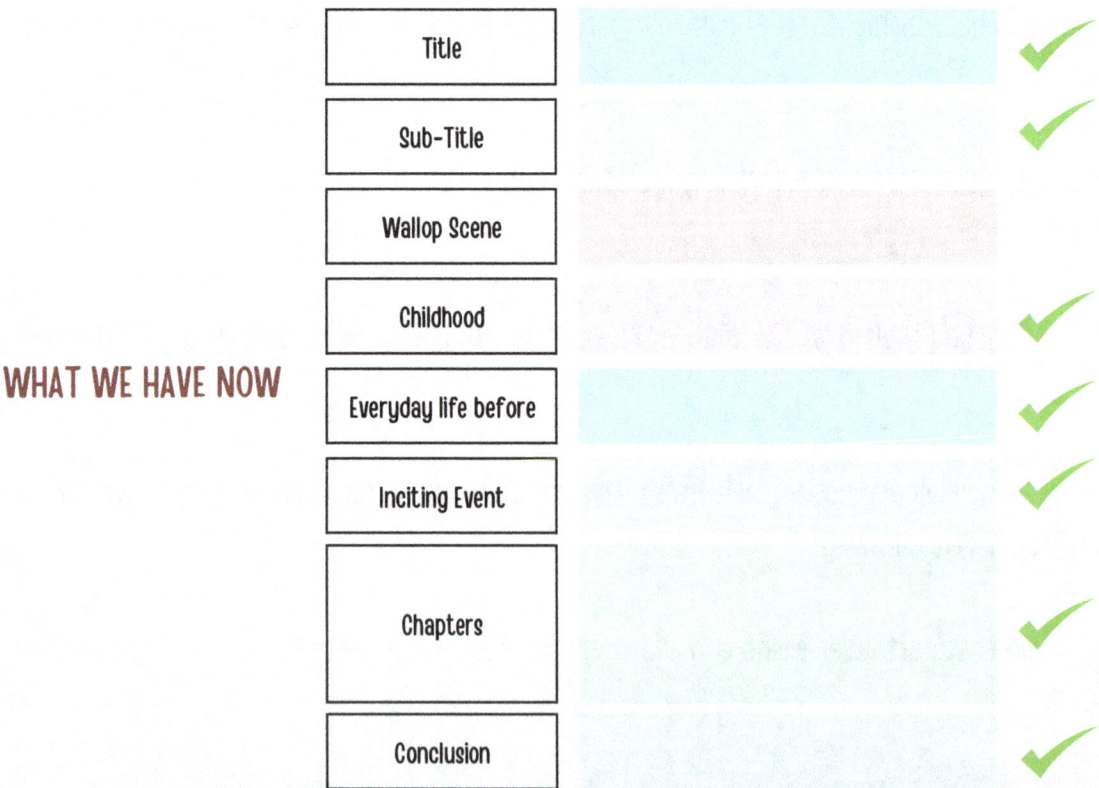

The Structure of Your Memoir
'The Building Blocks'

WHAT WE HAVE NOW

- Title ✓
- Sub-Title ✓
- Wallop Scene
- Childhood ✓
- Everyday life before ✓
- Inciting Event ✓
- Chapters ✓
- Conclusion ✓

NOW TURN TO PAGE 180 FOR YOUR END-OF-UNIT ACTIVITY 'YOUR TURN 17' PAGE:

'YOUR MEMOIR OUTLINE'

THE WALLOP SCENE

THE WALLOP SCENE

In this section, you will say goodbye to boring beginnings and hello to a dramatic opening that leaves your readers breathless... using a VERY simple tactic.

WHAT IS A WALLOP SCENE?

It's a phrase we coined. It's the part that makes you go 'Whoaa!!'

It IMMEDIATELY hooks the reader in.

It is super easy to do and we will show you how.

A little secret - you have ALREADY created it!

You see 'wallop' scenes everywhere without realising it...

If you watch a crime documentary, it is common for it to start with a scene saying:

"Police please! I think somebody is in my house!"

Its job is to hook the viewer in - and it works.

It will then rewind back to before the incident to show how it built up to that scene.

LET'S LOOK AT AN EXAMPLE

Let's look at a pretend scene from our Mount Everest memoir.

This one was picked because it was particularly dramatic.

THE WALLOP SCENE

KEY SCENE/STEP: SUMMIT CLIMB

The wind howled ferociously, whipping snow into my face and stinging my eyes as I clung to the icy rock. My fingers, numb from the cold, struggled to find purchase. The scent of the mountain, a mix of earth and ice, filled my nostrils. "Keep moving, John!" yelled Sarah, her voice barely audible over the roaring wind. Each breath was a searing gulp of thin air, and my muscles burned with exhaustion.

Suddenly, I felt a sharp crack beneath my feet, followed by a sickening lurch. The ice was giving way. "John, watch out!" Sarah screamed, panic threading her voice. My heart pounded as I scrambled to find a stable hold, the taste of fear bitter on my tongue. We were in big trouble.

The summit, so tantalisingly close, now seemed impossibly far as the icy ground betrayed me.

Highlighted in red is everything we think would make a great 'Wallop scene'. We've started with action and stopped it without revealing how they would get out of trouble – WE DON'T WANT TO GIVE AWAY SPOILERS DO WE?

The wind howled ferociously, whipping snow into my face and stinging my eyes as I clung to the icy rock. My fingers, numb from the cold, struggled to find purchase. The scent of the mountain, a mix of earth and ice, filled my nostrils. "Keep moving, John!" yelled Sarah, her voice barely audible over the roaring wind. Each breath was a searing gulp of thin air, and my muscles burned with exhaustion.

Suddenly, I felt a sharp crack beneath my feet, followed by a sickening lurch. The ice was giving way. "John, watch out!" Sarah screamed, panic threading her voice. My heart pounded as I scrambled to find a stable hold, the taste of fear bitter on my tongue. We were in big trouble.

The summit, so tantalisingly close, now seemed impossibly far as the icy ground betrayed me.

THE WALLOP SCENE

MY WALLOP SCENE IS:

The scent of the mountain, a mix of earth and ice, filled my nostrils. "Keep moving, John!" yelled Sarah, her voice barely audible over the roaring wind. Each breath was a searing gulp of thin air, and my muscles burned with exhaustion.

Suddenly, I felt a sharp crack beneath my feet, followed by a sickening lurch. The ice was giving way. "John, watch out!" Sarah screamed, panic threading her voice. My heart pounded as I scrambled to find a stable hold, the taste of fear bitter on my tongue.

We were in big trouble.

Your reader will be hooked!

- We have left our reader breathless.

- We haven't given away any spoilers.

- We don't say if we all got out of it.

- We don't say how.

They will have to keep reading to find out...

Which means we have them hooked!

THE WALLOP SCENE

KEY TAKEAWAYS

- **Immediate danger:** Starting with an intense moment, like a climber losing their grip on a cliff edge, grabs the reader's attention right away. This hooks the reader by creating a sense of urgency and stakes from the very beginning.

- **Hint of conflict:** Introducing a problem or conflict, such as an unexpected storm rolling in, teases the challenges and struggles to come. This keeps readers engaged by making them curious about how the climber will overcome these obstacles.

- **Cliffhanger:** Ending the scene on a suspenseful note, like the climber hearing the ice crack beneath them, leaves readers desperate to find out what happens next. This ensures they stay hooked, eager to turn the page and continue the story.

WHAT WE HAVE NOW

The Structure of Your Memoir
'The Building Blocks'

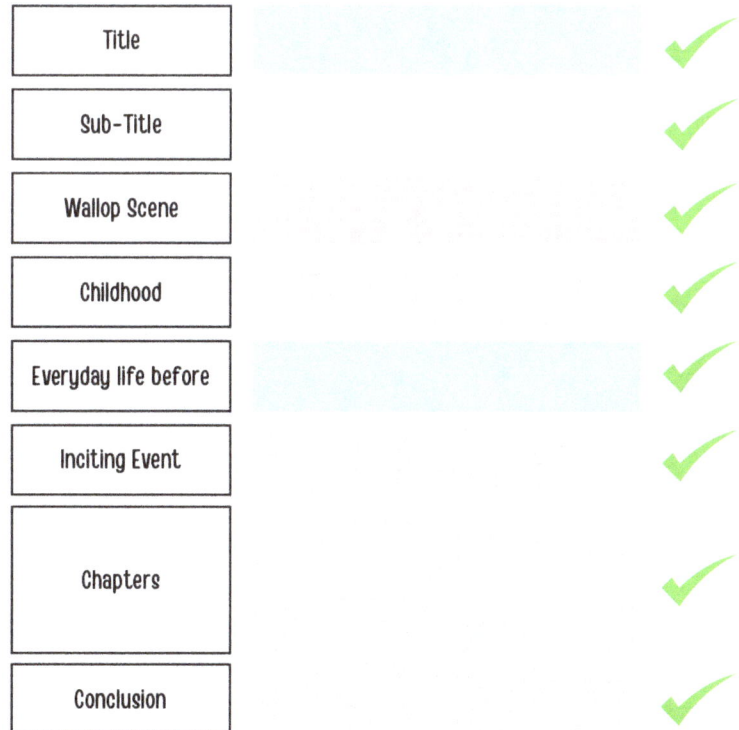

NOW TURN TO PAGE 220 FOR YOUR END-OF-UNIT ACTIVITY 'YOUR TURN 18' PAGE:

'YOUR WALLOP SCENE'

WRITE YOUR MEMOIR IN FULL

WRITE YOUR MEMOIR IN FULL

You now have all of the tools to write your memoir in full. Remember to use our structure (below) and your 12 step outline to help you with each chapter.

The Structure of Your Memoir
'The Building Blocks'

- Title ✓
- Sub-Title ✓
- Wallop Scene ✓
- Childhood ✓
- Everyday life before ✓
- Inciting Event ✓
- Chapters ✓
- Conclusion ✓

EDITING

EDITING

In this section, you will edit your memoir so that it has included all the important elements to create an immersive memoir.

WHAT ARE THE MOST IMPORTANT ELEMENTS?

Make sure you have included the following in every major scene:

Setting: I describe where and when the scene takes place to ground the reader in the story's environment. I include details such as time of day, location, and atmosphere.

Example: "The sun was setting over the rugged coastline, casting a golden hue on the crashing waves below."

♦

Characters: I introduce the characters involved in the scene and provide enough detail to make them believable and relatable. I show their actions, thoughts, and emotions to bring them to life.

Example: "I watched anxiously as my son, Adam, climbed the tree with determined focus, his face flushed with excitement."

♦

Dialogue: I use dialogue to reveal character personalities, advance the plot, and create tension or resolution. I make it natural and purposeful, reflecting how people speak.

Example: "I'm not sure I can do this."

♦

Action: I depict actions and movements to show what characters are doing and how they interact with their surroundings. Action drives the scene forward and keeps readers engaged.

Example: "I reached out to steady the ladder as Adam climbed higher, my heart pounding with a mix of pride and fear."

EDITING

Sensory details: I engage the reader's senses by describing sights, sounds, smells, tastes, and textures. This creates a richer, more immersive experience.

<u>Example</u>: "The salty breeze carried the scent of seaweed and brine, while seagulls squawked overhead and waves crashed against the rocks."

Emotions: I show my internal thoughts and feelings to deepen emotional connections with readers. This adds depth and authenticity to the scene.

<u>Example</u>: "As Adam reached the top, I felt a surge of relief and admiration for my son's courage, mixed with a twinge of maternal worry."

TO SUMMARISE

For every major scene <u>ensure</u> you have included:

- Setting.

- Characters.

- Dialogue.

- Action.

- Emotions.

- Sensory details (see, hear, touch, taste, smell).

EDITING

When editing, <u>ensure</u> you do the following:

Spelling, punctuation, and grammar:

- Use spell check and proofread carefully for spelling errors.
- Check punctuation (commas, full stops, etc.) for accuracy and consistency.
- Ensure grammar is correct.

Dialogue:

- Start a new line for each new speaker to clarify who is talking.
- Use quotation marks (" ") around spoken words.
- Punctuate dialogue correctly, including commas, full stops, question marks, and exclamation points inside the quotation marks as needed.

Websites for help:

- Grammarly: Offers grammar and spell check, and suggestions for sentence structure.

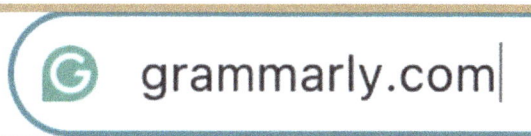

- Hemingway Editor: Highlights complex sentences and offers readability scores.

EDITING

CHECKLIST

Use the checklist below to make sure you have thought about each element in the final draft of your memoir.

DO	DON'T	CHECKED?
The theme - that it's encouraging	Depressing (Make it more cheery)	
Beautifully written	Impossible to believe (far-fetched) (Make it more believable)	
Eye-opening	Victim mentality throughout (Make it more about surviving)	
Vivid storytelling/Imagery	Negative (Make it more of a positive experience)	
Raw and painful	No self-reflection (Reflect on your own behaviour)	
Uplifting/inspiring	No mention of flaws (Mention when you've been wrong)	
Can-do attitude	Offensive (Ensuring it is an inclusive read - no offence)	
Funny/sad in places	Boring (Make it interesting)	

YOUR NEXT STEPS

YOUR NEXT STEPS

In this section, you will discover the different options you have now that you've written your memoir.

SOME IDEAS FOR YOU TO THINK ABOUT

Prepare your memoir for publishing:

- **Edit and polish:** Make sure your memoir is clear and error-free. You might want to get feedback from friends or a writing group.

- **Choose how to publish:** Decide if you want to find a literary agent and traditional publisher or self-publish using platforms like Amazon.

- **Design your book cover:** Create or hire someone to design an eye-catching cover and format the interior professionally. We have used Canva.com to do some covers ourselves and we have used Fiverr.com for designers.

Build your presence and market your memoir:

- **Create an author platform:** Start a simple website and set up social media profiles (like Facebook, Instagram, and X (formerly Twitter)).

- **Share your story:** Write blog posts about the themes in your memoir and share snippets or behind-the-scenes stories.

- **Connect with readers:** Engage with your audience by responding to comments and messages. Ask questions to create conversations around your memoir topic.

- **Get reviews:** Ask friends, family, and early readers for reviews. Positive reviews can help attract more readers.

YOUR NEXT STEPS

Prepare to speak about your memoir:

- Find speaking opportunities: Look for local libraries, bookstores, or community groups that host author talks.

- Create your presentation: Develop a short, engaging talk about your memoir's themes or your writing journey. Practise speaking it aloud. (We use canva.com for slides/presentations)

- Promote your talks: Use your website and social media to announce your speaking engagements. Consider making flyers or posters to put up locally. We use canva.com to create the flyers (they have ready-made templates and then we use Instant Print to print flyers).

Explore business opportunities:

- Identify your strengths: Consider offering workshops or mentoring sessions based on your experiences in writing your memoir. Think about a 'How-to' type workshop. (How to prepare for a climbing expedition)

    - SOME EXAMPLES:
        - 1. How to create a fulfilling relationship.
        - 2. How to build a successful business.
        - 3. How to prepare for a climbing expedition.
        - 4. How to cope with and overcome grief.
        - 5. How to cultivate mental wellness.

- Create additional products: Design merchandise related to your memoir (like bookmarks or posters) that you can sell alongside your book.

- Collaborate: Partner with local businesses or other authors for joint events or promotions.

YOUR NEXT STEPS

FINAL THOUGHTS

Starting out as a writer and speaker can be exciting and challenging.

Remember to take things step by step, stay patient with yourself, and enjoy the journey of sharing your story with the world.

Good luck!

YOUR TURN PAGES

ACTIVITIES

YOUR TURN 1

WHAT YOU LIKE AND DISLIKE ABOUT MEMOIRS

YOUR TURN 1

Think about your own experience in reading memoirs.

WHAT YOU LIKED AND DISLIKED ABOUT MEMOIRS: LESSONS YOU LEARNED.

What did you like about the memoir? Be as specific as possible:

Why did you like those parts of the memoir? How did the author do this?:

Why did you dislike those parts of the memoir?:

What do you think the author learned from their experiences in the memoir?:

What do you wish the memoir had been like and why?:

What parts of the memoir made it great or not so great? (The beginning, end etc.?:

What feelings did the memoir make you have? (Were you inspired, or depressed?):

Would you recommend this memoir to someone else? Why or why not?:

YOUR TURN 2

WRITE 5 POSSIBLE IDEAS FOR YOUR MEMOIR

YOUR TURN 2

Write 5 possible ideas for your memoir.
(Think about the following:)

Biggest struggle	What was the hardest challenge you've ever faced?
Biggest achievement	What is your proudest moment?
Unusual experience	Have you ever had an experience that felt out of the ordinary?
Near-death experience	Have you ever been in a situation where you feared for your life?
Grief	Have you experienced the loss of someone close to you?
Life-changing decision	Have you ever made a decision that significantly altered the course of your life?
Personal transformation	Is there a time in your life when you felt you changed significantly?
Cultural or family traditions	Are there any cultural or family traditions that have deeply influenced you?
Love and relationships	Have you experienced a significant romantic relationship?
Travel and adventure	Have you ever travelled to a place that left a lasting impression on you?

YOUR TURN 2

MY FIVE IDEAS

1	
2	
3	
4	
5	

YOUR TURN 2

LET'S DIVE DEEPER...

IDEA 1 – : ....

Transformation: From: .... To: ....

Main lesson(s) I learned: ....

———— ♦ ————

IDEA 2 – : ....

Transformation: From: .... To: ....

Main lesson(s) I learned: ....

———— ♦ ————

IDEA 3 – : ....

Transformation: From: .... To: ....

Main lesson(s) I learned: ....

———— ♦ ————

IDEA 4 – : ....

Transformation: From: .... To: ....

Main lesson(s) I learned: ....

———— ♦ ————

IDEA 5 – : ....

Transformation: From: .... To: ....

Main lesson(s) I learned: ....

YOUR TURN 3

ANSWER THE FOLLOWING QUESTIONS ABOUT
EACH OF YOUR 5 MEMOIR IDEAS

YOUR TURN 3

ANSWER THE FOLLOWING QUESTIONS ABOUT EACH OF YOUR 5 MEMOIR IDEAS:

Question 1: How BIG is the transformation in this idea? (out of 10 - 10 being the BIGGEST transformation)

IDEA 1 - : .... Score out of 10: ....
IDEA 2 - : .... Score out of 10: ....
IDEA 3 - : .... Score out of 10: ....
IDEA 4 - : .... Score out of 10: ....
IDEA 5 - : .... Score out of 10: ....

HIGHEST SCORE: IDEA ....

Question 2: How much advice and how many lessons have I learned that I can pass on for each idea? (out of 10)

IDEA 1 - : .... Score out of 10: ....
IDEA 2 - : .... Score out of 10: ....
IDEA 3 - : .... Score out of 10: ....
IDEA 4 - : .... Score out of 10: ....
IDEA 5 - : .... Score out of 10: ....

HIGHEST SCORE: IDEA ....

Question 1: How much do I want to write this memoir? (mark each idea out of 10):

IDEA 1 - : .... Score out of 10: ....
IDEA 2 - : .... Score out of 10: ....
IDEA 3 - : .... Score out of 10: ....
IDEA 4 - : .... Score out of 10: ....
IDEA 5 - : .... Score out of 10: ....

HIGHEST SCORE: IDEA ....

IDEA NUMBER .... IS MY WINNER

YOUR TURN 4

THE "I'M READY" STATEMENT

YOUR TURN 4
THE "I'M READY" STATEMENT

Emotional readiness:

How do you feel about revisiting and exploring past experiences in your memoir?:

Have you thought about how you might manage strong emotions that could arise during the writing process?:

Clarity of reflection:

What lessons have you learned from your experiences that you want to share in your memoir?:

Can you describe how these experiences have shaped your life and perspective?:

Purpose and motivation:

Why do you want to write your memoir? What do you hope readers will gain from reading it?:

How does sharing your story benefit others or contribute to a larger conversation?:

Support system:

Who are the people in your life who can provide emotional support as you write your memoir?:

When will you know if you need to speak to them?:

WRITE THE WORDS "I'M READY TO WRITE MY MEMOIR ON THIS SUBJECT" (ONLY IF YOU FEEL READY)

YOUR TURN 5

FILL IN THE OVERVIEW FORM

YOUR TURN 5

Fill out the Overview form.

This will provide lots of answers for you when you come to write your memoir.

We know these are important.

Don't worry about putting them in chronological order just write the ideas as they come into your head.

We will sort the order later.

OVERVIEW

Purpose:
Why are you writing this memoir? Is it to share your experiences, teach lessons, or simply tell your story?:
....
....
....
....

Theme:
What is the central theme or message of your memoir? It could be overcoming adversity, personal growth, finding identity, etc:
....
....
....

Personal growth:
Highlight key moments of change and transformation in your life. These can be gradual or sudden shifts in your perspective, behaviour, or circumstances.
....
....
....

YOUR TURN 5

Turning point:

Identify significant turning points that had a profound impact on your life direction:
....
....
....

Life lessons:

Share the most important lessons you've learned throughout your life. These can be about love, loss, resilience, happiness, etc.
....
....
....

Advice:

Offer advice or insights that others can learn from your experiences.
....
....
....

Key locations

Describe the various settings where important events took place. This could include your hometown, places you travelled to, schools, workplaces, etc.
....
....
....

Pivotal moments:

Include vivid and detailed descriptions of specific memories that were pivotal in your life. These could be joyful, painful, or transformative.
....
....
....

Key people:

Describe the important people in your life - family, friends, mentors, adversaries - and their influence on you.
....
....
....

YOUR TURN 5

Obstacles:
Detail the challenges and obstacles you've faced. How did you overcome them? What did you learn from these experiences?

Internal conflicts:
IReflect on any internal struggles or conflicts you faced, such as doubts, fears, or moral dilemmas.

Self reflection:
Engage in self-reflection to analyse your actions, choices, and their consequences. This introspection helps to provide depth and honesty.

Growth and change:
Reflect on how you have grown and changed over time. What insights have you gained about yourself and life?

Vulnerability:
Don't shy away from showing vulnerability. Sharing your weaknesses and failures can be just as powerful as your successes.

YOUR TURN 6

YOUR READER AVATAR

YOUR TURN 6

This is about YOU (But with THEM in mind)

You will create a simplified version of what your memoir is about but with your reader avatar in mind.

This can be used as an elevator pitch (something you say to somebody quickly if they ask what your memoir is about), or for sales purposes - ads etc.

My memoir about (Your subject matter - Climbing Everest): ....
....

It will help (gender) .... aged .... who are interested in (themes) ....
....

by sharing how I (main goal) ....
....

by overcoming (main problem) ....
....

EXAMPLE

My memoir about Climbing Everest helps adult men aged 25-45, who are interested in adventure and perseverance.

It shares how I achieved my dream of reaching the summit of Everest, showing how I overcame the challenges of physical exhaustion and looking death in the face.

WRITE YOUR VERSION IN FULL HERE:

YOUR TURN 7

YOUR INCITING EVENT

146

YOUR TURN 7

1: Write down the situation/context when you knew your life had changed.

Include who was there, what time, how you felt, dialogue etc...

2: Highlight/circle the actual POINT when your life changed – THIS IS THE INCITING EVENT

3: Write your Inciting Event in one simple sentence.

My Inciting Event is/was: (No more than one sentence):

YOUR TURN 8

YOUR HOOKY QUESTION

YOUR TURN 8

Write your Inciting Event line here:

Write how you felt about it in 1-3 words:

What main obstacle would you face?:

Now write that obstacle as a 'hooky' question:

HOOKY QUESTION:
WRITE ALL THE ABOVE AS A SHORT PARAGRAPH HERE:

YOUR TURN 9

YOUR 'MOMENTS BEFORE'

YOUR TURN 9

Write your 'MOMENTS BEFORE' (YOU WROTE THIS ON 'YOUR TURN 7') in slightly more detail.

- Add some dialogue (if relevant).
- Add some of the 5 senses (see, hear, touch, taste, smell).
- Add who was there.
- Add where you were.
- In general, what was life like?
- How did you feel about life at this point and why?

YOUR TURN 10

PUTTING THEM ALL TOGETHER

YOUR TURN 10

Put it all together in order – tweak slightly if necessary.

1 – Write the 'Moments before' the Inciting Event (CONTENT IS ON 'YOUR TURN 9')

2 – Write the Inciting Event (CONTENT IS ON 'YOUR TURN 7')

3 – Write the 'Hooky question' (CONTENT IS ON 'YOUR TURN 8')

YOUR
TURN 11

EVERYDAY LIFE 2-3 YEARS BEFORE THE INCITING EVENT

YOUR TURN 11

What was my 'Inciting Event?' - ONE sentence to remind me:
....
....
....
....

Write about your EVERYDAY LIFE BEFORE the 'Inciting Event' (around 2-3 years BEFORE)

Simple prompts for writing about your life before the 'Inciting Event':

WHAT TO INCLUDE

Daily routine: Describe your typical day. What did you do? Who did you spend time with? Where did you go?

Emotions: How did you feel during this time? Were you happy, content, bored, or worried about something?

Important relationships: Who were the key people in your life? Family, friends, colleagues?

Personal goals: What were your goals or dreams before the event? What were you working towards or hoping for?

Setting: Describe the places that were important to you. Your home, workplace, favourite hangout spots.

YOUR TURN 11

Daily routine: Describe your typical day. What did you do? Who did you spend time with? Where did you go?:
....
....
....

Emotions: How did you feel during this time? Were you happy, content, bored, or worried about something?:
....
....
....

Important relationships: Who were the key people in your life? Family, friends, colleagues?:
....
....
....

Personal goals: What were your goals or dreams before the event? What were you working towards or hoping for?
....
....
....

Setting: Describe the places that were important to you. Your home, workplace, and favourite hangout spots:
....
....
....

YOUR TURN 11

NOW WRITE IT ALL UP IN A READABLE PARAGRAPH

Start with 'I'

YOUR TURN 12

YOUR CHILDHOOD

YOUR TURN 12

When and where were you born?:

What are your earliest memories?:

Who were the key people in your early life (family, caregivers, friends)?:

What was your family dynamic like (parents' occupations, siblings, family traditions)?:

Where did you grow up (describe your hometown or neighbourhood)?:

What schools did you attend? Any memorable teachers or classmates?:

YOUR TURN 12

What were your favourite childhood activities or hobbies?:
....
....
....

Did you have any significant childhood challenges or obstacles?:
....
....
....

What were your dreams or aspirations as a child?:
....
....
....

How did your family celebrate holidays and special occasions?:
....
....
....

Were there any pivotal moments or events during your childhood that shaped who you are today?:
....
....
....

Describe your relationship with your siblings (if any) and how it influenced your upbringing:
....
....

YOUR TURN 12

What were some of the rules or values your parents emphasised while you were growing up?:
....
....
....

How did your cultural or religious background influence your childhood experiences?:
....
....
....

What were some of the places you loved visiting as a child (parks, libraries, favourite spots)?:
....
....
....

What was your wildest dream as a kid and why?:
....
....
....

YOUR TURN 13

YOUR 12 STEPS

YOUR TURN 13

1 - Write your FIRST step just after the inciting event. (What was the VERY NEXT THING you did JUST AFTER your inciting event?):

2 - Write your LAST step when you knew the journey had finished:

3 - Brainstorm ALL the important steps in between (don't worry about the chronological order at first):

YOUR TURN 13

<u>4</u> - Now sort them into the most IMPORTANT 12 steps IN ORDER. Remove the lesser important steps:

STEP 1: ....

STEP 2: ....

STEP 3: ....

STEP 4: ....

STEP 5: ....

STEP 6: ....

STEP 7: ....

STEP 8: ....

STEP 9: ....

STEP 10: ....

STEP 11: ....

STEP 12: ....

YOUR TURN 14

FIRST, NEXT AND LAST

YOUR TURN 14

STEPS INTO CHAPTERS

STEP 1: Chapter Heading

    First, I did…

    Next, I did…

    The last thing I did…

STEP 2: Chapter Heading

    First, I did…

    Next, I did…

    The last thing I did…

STEP 3: Chapter Heading

    First, I did…

    Next, I did…

    The last thing I did…

YOUR TURN 14

STEPS INTO CHAPTERS

STEP 4: Chapter Heading

First, I did…

Next, I did…

The last thing I did…

STEP 5: Chapter Heading

First, I did…

Next, I did…

The last thing I did…

STEP 6: Chapter Heading

First, I did…

Next, I did…

The last thing I did…

YOUR TURN 14

STEPS INTO CHAPTERS

STEP 7: Chapter Heading

First, I did...

Next, I did...

The last thing I did...

STEP 8: Chapter Heading

First, I did...

Next, I did...

The last thing I did...

STEP 9: Chapter Heading

First, I did...

Next, I did...

The last thing I did...

YOUR TURN 14

STEPS INTO CHAPTERS

STEP 10: Chapter Heading

    First, I did…

    Next, I did…

    The last thing I did…

STEP 11: Chapter Heading

    First, I did…

    Next, I did…

    The last thing I did…

STEP 12: Chapter Heading

    First, I did…

    Next, I did…

    The last thing I did…

YOUR TURN 15

YOUR TITLE AND SUBTITLE

YOUR TURN 15

1: Brainstorm a list of COMMON words associated with your memoir. eg: 'The Wall' (climbing), 'Life in a Blue One' (Royal Navy):

2: Pick your favourite:

3: Look on Amazon in your genre, and write down 5-10 words associated with your memoir:

4: Pick your favourite. Play about with title ideas:

IDENTIFY CORE THEMES

Activity: Write down the main themes of your memoir.

Example: If your memoir is about overcoming personal challenges, list themes like resilience, healing, and transformation.

TIP: Think about the messages and emotions you want to convey to your readers.

'From being in a dead-end job to having the courage to serve on the front line'

YOUR TURN 15

HIGHLIGHT UNIQUE ASPECTS

Activity: List the unique aspects of your story.

Example: Surviving a near-fatal accident.

TIP: Focus on what sets your memoir apart from others.

....
....
....

USE POWERFUL, EVOCATIVE LANGUAGE

Activity: Combine the words and phrases from the previous step into potential titles.

Example: "Rising from the Ashes."

TIP: Avoid clichés and strive for originality.

....
....
....

CRAFT A SUBTITLE THAT PROVIDES CLARITY AND CONTEXT

Activity: Write a subtitle that clarifies the main title and gives more context about your memoir.

Example: "A Journey of Healing and Triumph After Tragedy."

....
....
....

YOUR TURN 15

FINAL TITLE AND SUBTITLE

Final Version: "Rising from the Ashes: A Journey of Healing and Triumph After Tragedy."

....
....
....
....

FILL-IN-THE-BLANKS FRAMEWORK FOR A MEMOIR TITLE AND SUBTITLE

Title: "_____ (strong, evocative word or phrase) from _____ (place, event, or situation)"

Subtitle: "A _____ (Adjective) Journey of _____ (theme/emotion) and _____ (theme/emotion)"

Example: Title: "Rising from the Ashes"

    Subtitle: "A Journey of Healing and Triumph After Tragedy."

TEMPLATE FOR YOUR USE:

Title: "_____ from _____"

Subtitle: "A _____ Journey of _____ and _____"

YOUR TURN 15

EXAMPLE 1

Theme: Resilience.

An important word I want to use?: Struggle.

Key experience: Overcoming a life-changing diagnosis.

Title: "Strength Through Struggle."

Subtitle: "A Journey of Resilience and Acceptance with Overcoming a Life-Changing Diagnosis"

Your title: ....

Your subtitle: ....

EXAMPLE 2

[Key experience/Theme]: A Memoir.

Example: "Surviving the Storm: A Memoir"

This straightforward format highlights a central experience or theme of the memoir.

[Key experience/Theme]: ....

[....]: ....

YOUR TURN 15

EXAMPLE 3

[Evocative Phrase/Metaphor]: A Story Of [Theme/Experience]

Example: "Whispers of the Heart: A Story of Love and Resilience"

This format uses an evocative phrase or metaphor to set the emotional tone, followed by a description of the central theme or experience.

[Evocative Phrase/Metaphor]: A Story Of [Theme/Experience] ....

[....................................]: .... [Theme/Experience] ....

EXAMPLE 4

[Adjective] [Noun]: [Theme/Experience]

Example: "Unbreakable Spirit: Conquering Adversity"

This format emphasises a characteristic or quality followed by a description of the central theme or experience.

[Adjective] [Noun]: .... [Theme/Experience] ....

[............] [............]   [............ / ....]

YOUR TURN 15

EXAMPLE 5

[Verb] [Noun] : [Theme/Experience]

Example: "Embracing Change: My Journey to Self-Discovery"

Using an action verb followed by a noun that represents a central theme or experience, capturing the dynamic nature of the memoir.

[Verb] [Noun] : .... **[Theme/Experience]** ....

[...............] [.....................] : [................... / ....] ....

EXAMPLE 6

[Personal Name/Identifier] : [Theme/Experience]

Example: "Anna's Song: A Memoir of Healing and Hope"

This format emphasises the personal connection of the author to the story, followed by a description of the central theme or experience.

[Person Name/Identifier]: .... **[Theme/Experience]** ....

[............. / ....]   [................ / ....] ....

YOUR TURN 16

YOUR LOGLINE

YOUR TURN 16

1: Write your name: ....

2: Write some descriptions about yourself: ....
....
....

3: Write the biggest obstacle you faced overall: ....
....
....

4: Write your biggest fear (internal worries): ....
....
....

5: Write the setting where this all takes place: ....
....
....

6: Write the goal you need to achieve: ....
....
....

7: Write why that goal needs to be achieved/Why does it matter so much?: ....
....
....

YOUR TURN 16

Template for you to use:

[Protagonist's Name], a [brief description of protagonist], [faces/conflicts with], [in location or setting], [and must achieve/overcome] to [stakes or consequences].

Example:

John, an ambitious mountaineer, faces crippling self-doubt and physical challenges while climbing the treacherous slopes of Mount Everest, and must conquer his inner fears to prove his worth and fulfill his lifelong dream of reaching the summit.

Your logline:

YOUR TURN 17

YOUR MEMOIR OUTLINE

FILL IN THE BLANKS

INTRODUCTION

Your title:

Your subtitle:

Your opening line/wallop scene: (DO THIS LAST)

Your childhood:

INTRODUCTION

Your childhood:

Everyday life before:

Inciting Event (including hooky question etc.)

CHAPTER 1

STEP 1 – What did you do FIRST?

The main thing that happened in this scene (for reference):

Setting (use 5 senses):

Characters involved in this scene?:

Action – What actually happened step-by-step?:

Dialogue – What was actually said and by whom?:

Conflict – What went wrong and why?:

Emotions – What did I feel and why?:

My internal thoughts:

Resolution – How did this scene end?:

Lesson(s) I learned and why?:

CHAPTER 1

STEP 1 - What did you do NEXT?

The main thing that happened in this scene (for reference): ....

Setting (use 5 senses): ....

Characters involved in this scene?: ....

Action - What actually happened step-by-step?: ....

Dialogue - What was actually said and by whom?: ....

Conflict - What went wrong and why?: ....

Emotions - What did I feel and why?: ....

My internal thoughts: ....

Resolution - How did this scene end?: ....

Lesson(s) I learned and why?: ....

CHAPTER 1

STEP 1 – What did you do LAST?

The main thing that happened in this scene (for reference): ....
....
....

Setting (use 5 senses): ....
....
....

Characters involved in this scene?: ....
....
....

Action – What actually happened step-by-step?: ....
....
....

Dialogue – What was actually said and by whom?: ....
....
....

Conflict – What went wrong and why?: ....
....
....

Emotions – What did I feel and why?: ....
....
....

My internal thoughts: ....
....
....

Resolution – How did this scene end?: ....
....
....

Lesson(s) I learned and why?: ....
....

CHAPTER 2

STEP 2 – What did you do FIRST?

The main thing that happened in this scene (for reference): ....
....
....

Setting (use 5 senses): ....
....
....

Characters involved in this scene?: ....
....
....

Action – What actually happened step-by-step?: ....
....
....

Dialogue – What was actually said and by whom?: ....
....
....

Conflict – What went wrong and why?: ....
....
....

Emotions – What did I feel and why?: ....
....
....

My internal thoughts: ....
....
....

Resolution – How did this scene end?: ....
....
....

Lesson(s) I learned and why?: ....
....

CHAPTER 2

Scene number 1 – **What did you do NEXT?**

The main thing that happened in this scene (for reference):

Setting (use 5 senses):

Characters involved in this scene?:

Action – What actually happened step-by-step?:

Dialogue – What was actually said and by whom?:

Conflict – What went wrong and why?:

Emotions – What did I feel and why?:

My internal thoughts:

Resolution – How did this scene end?:

Lesson(s) I learned and why?:

CHAPTER 2

Scene number 1 – **What did you do LAST?**

The main thing that happened in this scene (for reference): ....

Setting (use 5 senses): ....

Characters involved in this scene?: ....

Action – What actually happened step-by-step?: ....

Dialogue – What was actually said and by whom?: ....

Conflict – What went wrong and why?: ....

Emotions – What did I feel and why?: ....

My internal thoughts: ....

Resolution – How did this scene end?: ....

Lesson(s) I learned and why?: ....

CHAPTER 3

Scene number 1 - What did you do FIRST?

The main thing that happened in this scene (for reference): ....
....
....

Setting (use 5 senses): ....
....
....

Characters involved in this scene?: ....
....
....

Action - What actually happened step-by-step?: ....
....
....

Dialogue - What was actually said and by whom?: ....
....
....

Conflict - What went wrong and why?: ....
....
....

Emotions - What did I feel and why?: ....
....
....

My internal thoughts: ....
....
....

Resolution - How did this scene end?: ....
....
....

Lesson(s) I learned and why?: ....
....
....

CHAPTER 3

Scene number 1 - What did you do NEXT?

The main thing that happened in this scene (for reference): ....
....
....

Setting (use 5 senses): ....
....
....

Characters involved in this scene?: ....
....
....

Action - What actually happened step-by-step?: ....
....
....

Dialogue - What was actually said and by whom?: ....
....
....

Conflict - What went wrong and why?: ....
....
....

Emotions - What did I feel and why?: ....
....
....

My internal thoughts: ....
....
....

Resolution - How did this scene end?: ....
....
....

Lesson(s) I learned and why?: ....
....
....

CHAPTER 3

Scene number 1 – **What did you do LAST?**

The main thing that happened in this scene (for reference): ....
....
....

Setting (use 5 senses): ....
....
....

Characters involved in this scene?: ....
....
....

Action – What actually happened step-by-step?: ....
....
....

Dialogue – What was actually said and by whom?: ....
....
....

Conflict – What went wrong and why?: ....
....
....

Emotions – What did I feel and why?: ....
....
....

My internal thoughts: ....
....
....

Resolution – How did this scene end?: ....
....
....

Lesson(s) I learned and why?: ....
....
....

CHAPTER 4

Scene number 1 - What did you do FIRST?

The main thing that happened in this scene (for reference): ....
....
....

Setting (use 5 senses): ....
....
....

Characters involved in this scene?: ....
....
....

Action - What actually happened step-by-step?: ....
....
....

Dialogue - What was actually said and by whom?: ....
....
....

Conflict - What went wrong and why?: ....
....
....

Emotions - What did I feel and why?: ....
....
....

My internal thoughts: ....
....
....

Resolution - How did this scene end?: ....
....
....

Lesson(s) I learned and why?: ....
....
....

CHAPTER 4

Scene number 1 - What did you do NEXT?

The main thing that happened in this scene (for reference):
....
....

Setting (use 5 senses):
....
....

Characters involved in this scene?:
....
....

Action - What actually happened step-by-step?:
....
....

Dialogue - What was actually said and by whom?:
....
....

Conflict - What went wrong and why?:
....
....

Emotions - What did I feel and why?:
....
....

My internal thoughts:
....
....

Resolution - How did this scene end?:
....
....

Lesson(s) I learned and why?:
....
....

CHAPTER 4

Scene number 1 - **What did you do LAST?**

The main thing that happened in this scene (for reference): ....
....
....

Setting (use 5 senses): ....
....
....

Characters involved in this scene?: ....
....
....

Action - What actually happened step-by-step?: ....
....
....

Dialogue - What was actually said and by whom?: ....
....
....

Conflict - What went wrong and why?: ....
....
....

Emotions - What did I feel and why?: ....
....
....

My internal thoughts: ....
....
....

Resolution - How did this scene end?: ....
....
....

Lesson(s) I learned and why?: ....
....
....

CHAPTER 5

Scene number 1 – What did you do FIRST?

The main thing that happened in this scene (for reference):

Setting (use 5 senses):

Characters involved in this scene?:

Action – What actually happened step-by-step?:

Dialogue – What was actually said and by whom?:

Conflict – What went wrong and why?:

Emotions – What did I feel and why?:

My internal thoughts:

Resolution – How did this scene end?:

Lesson(s) I learned and why?:

CHAPTER 5

Scene number 1 - What did you do NEXT?

The main thing that happened in this scene (for reference): ....
....
....

Setting (use 5 senses): ....
....
....

Characters involved in this scene?: ....
....
....

Action - What actually happened step-by-step?: ....
....
....

Dialogue - What was actually said and by whom?: ....
....
....

Conflict - What went wrong and why?: ....
....
....

Emotions - What did I feel and why?: ....
....
....

My internal thoughts: ....
....
....

Resolution - How did this scene end?: ....
....
....

Lesson(s) I learned and why?: ....
....
....

CHAPTER 5

Scene number 1 - What did you do <u>LAST?</u>

The main thing that happened in this scene (for reference):

Setting (use 5 senses):

Characters involved in this scene?:

Action - What actually happened step-by-step?:

Dialogue - What was actually said and by whom?:

Conflict - What went wrong and why?:

Emotions - What did I feel and why?:

My internal thoughts:

Resolution - How did this scene end?:

Lesson(s) I learned and why?:

CHAPTER 6

Scene number 1 - What did you do FIRST?

The main thing that happened in this scene (for reference): ....
....
....

Setting (use 5 senses): ....
....
....

Characters involved in this scene?: ....
....
....

Action - What actually happened step-by-step?: ....
....
....

Dialogue - What was actually said and by whom?: ....
....
....

Conflict - What went wrong and why?: ....
....
....

Emotions - What did I feel and why?: ....
....
....

My internal thoughts: ....
....
....

Resolution - How did this scene end?: ....
....
....

Lesson(s) I learned and why?: ....
....
....

CHAPTER 6

Scene number 1 – **What did you do NEXT?**

The main thing that happened in this scene (for reference):
....
....

Setting (use 5 senses):
....
....

Characters involved in this scene?:
....
....

Action – What actually happened step-by-step?:
....
....

Dialogue – What was actually said and by whom?:
....
....

Conflict – What went wrong and why?:
....
....

Emotions – What did I feel and why?:
....
....

My internal thoughts:
....
....

Resolution – How did this scene end?:
....
....

Lesson(s) I learned and why?:
....
....

CHAPTER 6

Scene number 1 - What did you do LAST?

The main thing that happened in this scene (for reference): ....
....
....

Setting (use 5 senses): ....
....
....

Characters involved in this scene?: ....
....
....

Action - What actually happened step-by-step?: ....
....
....

Dialogue - What was actually said and by whom?: ....
....
....

Conflict - What went wrong and why?: ....
....
....

Emotions - What did I feel and why?: ....
....
....

My internal thoughts: ....
....
....

Resolution - How did this scene end?: ....
....
....

Lesson(s) I learned and why?: ....
....

CHAPTER 7

Scene number 1 - What did you do FIRST?

The main thing that happened in this scene (for reference): ....

Setting (use 5 senses): ....

Characters involved in this scene?: ....

Action - What actually happened step-by-step?: ....

Dialogue - What was actually said and by whom?: ....

Conflict - What went wrong and why?: ....

Emotions - What did I feel and why?: ....

My internal thoughts: ....

Resolution - How did this scene end?: ....

Lesson(s) I learned and why?: ....

CHAPTER 7

Scene number 1 – What did you do NEXT?

The main thing that happened in this scene (for reference): ....
....
....

Setting (use 5 senses): ....
....
....

Characters involved in this scene?: ....
....
....

Action – What actually happened step-by-step?: ....
....
....

Dialogue – What was actually said and by whom?: ....
....
....

Conflict – What went wrong and why?: ....
....
....

Emotions – What did I feel and why?: ....
....
....

My internal thoughts: ....
....
....

Resolution – How did this scene end?: ....
....
....

Lesson(s) I learned and why?: ....
....

CHAPTER 7

Scene number 1 – What did you do LAST?

The main thing that happened in this scene (for reference): ....
....
....

Setting (use 5 senses): ....
....
....

Characters involved in this scene?: ....
....
....

Action – What actually happened step-by-step?: ....
....
....

Dialogue – What was actually said and by whom?: ....
....
....

Conflict – What went wrong and why?: ....
....
....

Emotions – What did I feel and why?: ....
....
....

My internal thoughts: ....
....
....

Resolution – How did this scene end?: ....
....
....

Lesson(s) I learned and why?: ....
....
....

CHAPTER 8

Scene number 1 - What did you do FIRST?

The main thing that happened in this scene (for reference):

Setting (use 5 senses):

Characters involved in this scene?:

Action - What actually happened step-by-step?:

Dialogue - What was actually said and by whom?:

Conflict - What went wrong and why?:

Emotions - What did I feel and why?:

My internal thoughts:

Resolution - How did this scene end?:

Lesson(s) I learned and why?:

CHAPTER 8

Scene number 1 - What did you do NEXT?

The main thing that happened in this scene (for reference):

Setting (use 5 senses):

Characters involved in this scene?:

Action - What actually happened step-by-step?:

Dialogue - What was actually said and by whom?:

Conflict - What went wrong and why?:

Emotions - What did I feel and why?:

My internal thoughts:

Resolution - How did this scene end?:

Lesson(s) I learned and why?:

CHAPTER 8

Scene number 1 - What did you do LAST?

The main thing that happened in this scene (for reference): ....
....
....

Setting (use 5 senses): ....
....
....

Characters involved in this scene?: ....
....
....

Action - What actually happened step-by-step?: ....
....
....

Dialogue - What was actually said and by whom?: ....
....
....

Conflict - What went wrong and why?: ....
....
....

Emotions - What did I feel and why?: ....
....
....

My internal thoughts: ....
....
....

Resolution - How did this scene end?: ....
....
....

Lesson(s) I learned and why?: ....
....

CHAPTER 9

Scene number 1 – What did you do <u>FIRST?</u>

The main thing that happened in this scene (for reference): ....
....
....

Setting (use 5 senses): ....
....
....

Characters involved in this scene?: ....
....
....

Action – What actually happened step-by-step?: ....
....
....

Dialogue – What was actually said and by whom?: ....
....
....

Conflict – What went wrong and why?: ....
....
....

Emotions – What did I feel and why?: ....
....
....

My internal thoughts: ....
....
....

Resolution – How did this scene end?: ....
....
....

Lesson(s) I learned and why?: ....
....
....

CHAPTER 9

Scene number 1 - What did you do NEXT?

The main thing that happened in this scene (for reference): ....
....
....

Setting (use 5 senses): ....
....
....

Characters involved in this scene?: ....
....
....

Action - What actually happened step-by-step?: ....
....
....

Dialogue - What was actually said and by whom?: ....
....
....

Conflict - What went wrong and why?: ....
....
....

Emotions - What did I feel and why?: ....
....
....

My internal thoughts: ....
....
....

Resolution - How did this scene end?: ....
....
....

Lesson(s) I learned and why?: ....
....

CHAPTER 9

Scene number 1 - **What did you do LAST?**

The main thing that happened in this scene (for reference):

Setting (use 5 senses):

Characters involved in this scene?:

Action - What actually happened step-by-step?:

Dialogue - What was actually said and by whom?:

Conflict - What went wrong and why?:

Emotions - What did I feel and why?:

My internal thoughts:

Resolution - How did this scene end?:

Lesson(s) I learned and why?:

CHAPTER 10

Scene number 1 – What did you do FIRST?

The main thing that happened in this scene (for reference): ....
....
....

Setting (use 5 senses): ....
....
....

Characters involved in this scene?: ....
....
....

Action – What actually happened step-by-step?: ....
....
....

Dialogue – What was actually said and by whom?: ....
....
....

Conflict – What went wrong and why?: ....
....
....

Emotions – What did I feel and why?: ....
....
....

My internal thoughts: ....
....
....

Resolution – How did this scene end?: ....
....
....

Lesson(s) I learned and why?: ....
....
....

CHAPTER 10

Scene number 1 - What did you do NEXT?

The main thing that happened in this scene (for reference):

Setting (use 5 senses):

Characters involved in this scene?:

Action - What actually happened step-by-step?:

Dialogue - What was actually said and by whom?:

Conflict - What went wrong and why?:

Emotions - What did I feel and why?:

My internal thoughts:

Resolution - How did this scene end?:

Lesson(s) I learned and why?:

CHAPTER 10

Scene number 1 - What did you do LAST?

The main thing that happened in this scene (for reference): ....
....
....

Setting (use 5 senses): ....
....
....

Characters involved in this scene?: ....
....
....

Action - What actually happened step-by-step?: ....
....
....

Dialogue - What was actually said and by whom?: ....
....
....

Conflict - What went wrong and why?: ....
....
....

Emotions - What did I feel and why?: ....
....
....

My internal thoughts: ....
....
....

Resolution - How did this scene end?: ....
....
....

Lesson(s) I learned and why?: ....
....

CHAPTER 11

Scene number 1 - **What did you do FIRST?**

The main thing that happened in this scene (for reference): ....
....
....

Setting (use 5 senses): ....
....
....

Characters involved in this scene?: ....
....
....

Action - What actually happened step-by-step?: ....
....
....

Dialogue - What was actually said and by whom?: ....
....
....

Conflict - What went wrong and why?: ....
....
....

Emotions - What did I feel and why?: ....
....
....

My internal thoughts: ....
....
....

Resolution - How did this scene end?: ....
....
....

Lesson(s) I learned and why?: ....
....

CHAPTER 11

Scene number 1 - What did you do NEXT?

The main thing that happened in this scene (for reference): ....
....
....

Setting (use 5 senses): ....
....
....

Characters involved in this scene?: ....
....
....

Action - What actually happened step-by-step?: ....
....
....

Dialogue - What was actually said and by whom?: ....
....
....

Conflict - What went wrong and why?: ....
....
....

Emotions - What did I feel and why?: ....
....
....

My internal thoughts: ....
....
....

Resolution - How did this scene end?: ....
....
....

Lesson(s) I learned and why?: ....
....
....

CHAPTER 11

Scene number 1 - **What did you do LAST?**

The main thing that happened in this scene (for reference): ....
....
....

Setting (use 5 senses): ....
....
....

Characters involved in this scene?: ....
....
....

Action - What actually happened step-by-step?: ....
....
....

Dialogue - What was actually said and by whom?: ....
....
....

Conflict - What went wrong and why?: ....
....
....

Emotions - What did I feel and why?: ....
....
....

My internal thoughts: ....
....
....

Resolution - How did this scene end?: ....
....
....

Lesson(s) I learned and why?: ....
....

CHAPTER 12

Scene number 1 - What did you do FIRST?

The main thing that happened in this scene (for reference): ....
....
....

Setting (use 5 senses): ....
....
....

Characters involved in this scene?: ....
....
....

Action - What actually happened step-by-step?: ....
....
....

Dialogue - What was actually said and by whom?: ....
....
....

Conflict - What went wrong and why?: ....
....
....

Emotions - What did I feel and why?: ....
....
....

My internal thoughts: ....
....
....

Resolution - How did this scene end?: ....
....
....

Lesson(s) I learned and why?: ....
....
....

CHAPTER 12

Scene number 1 - What did you do NEXT?

The main thing that happened in this scene (for reference):

Setting (use 5 senses):

Characters involved in this scene?:

Action - What actually happened step-by-step?:

Dialogue - What was actually said and by whom?:

Conflict - What went wrong and why?:

Emotions - What did I feel and why?:

My internal thoughts:

Resolution - How did this scene end?:

Lesson(s) I learned and why?:

CHAPTER 12

Scene number 1 - What did you do LAST?

The main thing that happened in this scene (for reference): ....

Setting (use 5 senses): ....

Characters involved in this scene?: ....

Action - What actually happened step-by-step?: ....

Dialogue - What was actually said and by whom?: ....

Conflict - What went wrong and why?: ....

Emotions - What did I feel and why?: ....

My internal thoughts: ....

Resolution - How did this scene end?: ....

Lesson(s) I learned and why?: ....

CONCLUSION

Conclusion/advice:

Notes:

YOUR
TURN 18

YOUR WALLOP SCENE

220

YOUR TURN 18

You've written your 12-step outline.

<u>STEP 1</u> - Select the MOST dramatic of steps/scenes.

Read through it and ONLY circle the part where the action really starts and where it ALMOST ends (VERY IMPORTANT - we don't want to give away spoilers do we?)

THIS is now your wallop scene.

Add it into your structure.

RESOURCES

QUESTIONS AND ANSWERS

RESOURCES

WritersDigest.com: Features articles, prompts, and writing tips specifically for memoir and non-fiction writers.

WRITING TOOLS

Scrivener: A powerful content-generation tool for long documents, perfect for organising a memoir.

Evernote: A note-taking app that can help you organise thoughts, research, and drafts in one place.

Grammarly: An online writing assistant that can help with grammar, style, and readability.

WRITING GROUPS AND WORKSHOPS

National Association of Memoir Writers (NAMW): Offers membership for access to workshops, teleconferences, and a supportive community of memoir writers.

Meetup.com: Search for local or online memoir writing groups to join for peer support and feedback.

Local Libraries and Community Centres: Often host writing workshops and classes that can provide support and feedback.

RESOURCES

INSPIRATIONAL MEMOIRS TO READ

"Educated" by Tara Westover: A memoir about a woman who grows up in a strict and abusive household in rural Idaho but eventually escapes to learn about the wider world through education.

"Becoming" by Michelle Obama: An intimate, powerful, and inspiring memoir by the former First Lady of the United States.

"The Glass Castle" by Jeannette Walls: A memoir about a girl who grows up in a deeply dysfunctional family but finds the strength to carve out a successful life on her own terms.

TIPS ON MEMOIR WRITING

Be honest and authentic: Your story should reflect your true experiences and emotions.

Focus on themes: Identify key themes in your life and build your narrative around them.

Show, don't just tell: Use descriptive language to create vivid scenes that draw readers into your story.

Edit ruthlessly: Be prepared to revise and cut parts of your story to keep it engaging and concise.

ADDITIONAL SUPPORT

Writing coaches: Consider hiring a writing coach for personalised guidance and feedback on your memoir.

Beta readers: Seek out trusted friends, family, or fellow writers to read your drafts and provide constructive feedback.

Professional editors: Hiring a professional editor can help refine your memoir and ensure it's polished and ready for publication.

QUESTIONS AND ANSWERS

1. What is a memoir?

Answer: A memoir is a true story about your own life, focusing on specific themes or periods.

2. How is a memoir different from an autobiography?

Answer: An autobiography covers your entire life, while a memoir focuses on specific parts or themes.

3. Where do I start my memoir?

Answer: Start with a memorable moment or event that fits the theme you want to explore.

4. How do I choose what to include?

Answer: Include events and details that support the main theme or message of your memoir.

5. What themes can I write about?

Answer: Themes can be anything important to you, like family, love, loss, growth, or adventure.

6. How do I make my memoir interesting?

Answer: Use vivid descriptions, emotions, and dialogue to bring your story to life.

7. How honest should I be?

Answer: Be as honest as you can, but be respectful of others' privacy and feelings.

8. Can I change names and details?

Answer: Yes, you can change names and minor details to protect people's privacy.

9. How do I write about painful experiences?

Answer: Write with honesty and sensitivity, focusing on your feelings and growth.

QUESTIONS AND ANSWERS

10. How do I get started with writing?

Answer: Set aside regular time to write, even if it's just a few minutes a day.

11. What should my writing routine be?

Answer: Find a time and place where you can write regularly and without distractions.

12. How do I structure my memoir?

Answer: You can use chronological order, thematic sections, or flashbacks to structure your memoir.

13. How do I create vivid scenes?

Answer: Use sensory details (sight, sound, smell, touch, taste) and specific descriptions.

14. How do I show emotions in my writing?

Answer: Describe how you felt and how your body reacted to events (e.g., tears, shaking).

15. How do I write dialogue?

Answer: Write dialogue as if people are speaking naturally, but keep it relevant to the story.

16. How do I find my writing voice?

Answer: Write as you speak, and let your personality come through in your words.

17. How do I stay motivated?

Answer: Set small goals, celebrate progress, and remind yourself why you're writing.

QUESTIONS AND ANSWERS

18. How do I deal with writer's block?

Answer: Take breaks, try freewriting, or change your writing environment.

19. How much should I write each day?

Answer: Write as much as you can comfortably manage, even if it's just a few sentences.

20. How do I edit my work?

Answer: Take breaks between writing and editing, and read your work out loud to spot errors.

21. Should I get feedback from others?

Answer: Yes, getting feedback can help you see your work from different perspectives.

22. How do I handle negative feedback?

Answer: Use constructive feedback to improve, but stay true to your story.

23. How do I keep my reader engaged?

Answer: Keep your writing clear, concise, and focused on the story and emotions.

24. How long should my memoir be?

Answer: Aim for 60,000 to 100,000 words, but focus on telling your story well.

25. Do I need a professional editor?

Answer: A professional editor can help polish your work and catch errors you might miss.

26. How do I find a writing group?

Answer: Look for local groups at libraries or community centres, or join online writing communities.

QUESTIONS AND ANSWERS

27. How do I publish my memoir?

Answer: You can self-publish or submit to publishers; research both options to see what suits you best.

28. What should I do if I feel overwhelmed?

Answer: Break your writing into small, manageable tasks, and take it one step at a time.

29. How do I stay true to my voice and story?

Answer: Write from your heart, and remember that your unique perspective is valuable.

30. How do I handle sensitive topics?

Answer: Write with empathy and respect, and consider the impact on those involved.

31. Can I include photos or documents?

Answer: Yes, adding photos or documents can enhance your memoir and provide context.

32. How do I write about other people?

Answer: Be honest and fair, and get their permission if possible, especially for sensitive topics.

33. What if my memory isn't perfect?

Answer: It's okay to acknowledge that memories can be imperfect; focus on the essence of the story.

34. How do I find inspiration?

Answer: Read other memoirs, listen to music, or reflect on meaningful moments in your life.

35. How do I balance storytelling with reflection?

Answer: Mix scenes with your thoughts and feelings to provide depth and insight.

QUESTIONS AND ANSWERS

36. What are common mistakes to avoid?

Answer: Avoid writing too broadly, including unnecessary details, and neglecting to edit.

37. How do I handle legal issues?

Answer: If in doubt, consult a lawyer, especially when writing about sensitive or controversial topics.

38. How do I know if my story is worth telling?

Answer: Every story is worth telling if it has meaning to you and can resonate with others.

39. How do I write consistently?

Answer: Create a writing schedule and stick to it, even if it means writing a little each day.

40. What if I want to quit?

Answer: Remember why you started, take breaks if needed, and seek support from fellow writers.

41. How do I organise my notes and drafts?

Answer: Use tools like Scrivener, Evernote, or physical notebooks to keep everything in one place.

42. How do I deal with distractions?

Answer: Find a quiet place, turn off notifications, and set specific writing times.

43. How do I end my memoir?

Answer: End with a resolution or reflection that ties back to your main theme.

44. Can I use humour in my memoir?

Answer: Yes, humour can make your memoir more engaging, but use it appropriately.

QUESTIONS AND ANSWERS

45. How do I stay focused on my theme?

Answer: Keep reminding yourself of your main theme and cut anything that doesn't support it.

46. What if my story changes as I write?

Answer: That's okay; let your story evolve naturally and adjust your outline as needed.

47. How do I make my memoir relatable?

Answer: Share universal emotions and experiences that others can connect with.

48. Should I write in the past or present tense?

Answer: Choose the tense that feels most natural for your story; past tense is more common.

49. How do I avoid clichés?

Answer: Use your own unique voice and experiences, and avoid overused phrases and ideas.

50. What should I do after finishing my first draft?

Answer: Take a break, then start revising with fresh eyes, seeking feedback as needed.

CONGRATULATIONS!

You've written your memoir and it sounds brilliant!

www.ingramcontent.com/pod-product-compliance
Lightning Source LLC
Chambersburg PA
CBHW081615100526
44590CB00021B/3454